Taffs
at Home

IEUAN J SIMS

authorHOUSE®

AuthorHouse™ UK
1663 Liberty Drive
Bloomington, IN 47403 USA
www.authorhouse.co.uk
Phone: 0800.197.4150

Published by AuthorHouse 11/07/2018

ISBN: 978-1-7283-8049-0 (sc)
ISBN: 978-1-7283-8050-6 (e)

Library of Congress Control Number: 2018913310

Print information available on the last page.

To Rhian, Sophie, and Hayley

Contents

1

School and Tutor

Our local school was bombed almost beyond repair during the war at what was a crucial time for me—the period leading up to my scholarship exams. In some respects, my whole future could be said to depend on these. Was I to go to grammar school with the elite, to the technical college with the less intellectual but more practical, or to the unthinkable alternative—no school at all, facing the wide world at a very tender age? In the event, not having had the benefit of cramming in the final three months, I failed the exam.

My grandfather persuaded my shattered parents to stave off my fate by sending me to an accomplished though slightly eccentric uncle for tuition. With his assistance at 2s. 6d. an hour, it was hoped that I might yet attain a standard acceptable to a private school of good repute. From there, with an Oxford Senior School Certificate and credits to my name, university would still be a possibility.

To save the bus fare, so that I would have enough cash to go to the Regal Cinema on Saturday, I pushed myself to my first lesson on my old scooter. I introduced myself to Uncle's sister at the front door of Tyddewillansamlet.

I was ushered into a parlour and invited to sit down. The lady sitting opposite me, very erect in a frilly blouse and a skirt reaching to the floor, enquired of me which child of which of my grandmother's children I was, and what goal I had set myself in life. She then enquired after the health of my grandmother, Elisabeth Jane, and commented on what a fine figure of a woman she was, despite all the childbearing inflicted upon her.

Grandmother was a person of some quality from the eastern part of Carmarthenshire. She had reached the giddy heights of chief buyer for Lewis's Store and Salon, of London no less, and her name was familiar in such exotic places as New York and Paris. The lady seated with me expressed the hope that this quality might also show up in me with some grooming and a little luck.

I appeared to her to possess the basic requirements, as she had observed on opening her door to me, that my cap was on straight, my coat was properly buttoned, none of my shoelaces were undone, and I had addressed her correctly and politely. I had obviously refrained from aping that ghastly child called Just William, who currently had such bad influence among the nation's youth.

I was informed that my tutor was a highly respected man of substance. His first-class honours degree was from a famous university, and he had been third secretary at the British Legation in St Petersburg. Later he had been adjutant of an Indian regiment in the Punjab, prior to taking up his last appointment as one of the principal interpreters in

English, Hindi, Russian, *and* Esperanto at the League of Nations in Geneva, Switzerland.

Apparently, Uncle was also a skilful tutor who had amassed an enviable record getting senior college and university students through their exams. In the normal course of events, he would not have entertained such a menial task as coaching the likes of me. But as I was one of the family, he saw it as an obligation.

A tall, straight man with centre-parted, iron-grey hair and a ruddy complexion entered the room and shook my hand. Twirling his Kitchener moustache, he looked me over for a moment and then said with a grin, "No need to consult my diary over you, my lad. I can tell at a glance that you're a chip off the old block. D'you know what that means, hey?"

I hesitated, having heard the phrase somewhere but not quite being able to put it into words. I was in complete awe of him.

"Well, never mind. All will be revealed when we come to your English lessons. What? You're here for maths today, aren't you? Good! Good! Have you brought your two and six? Good! Very good! Now tell me, how many blue beans do you think make five, hey? And before you answer, don't forget the colour!"

"Five?" I ventured.

"What's that? Five! Good heavens, are you quite sure, boy?"

"Y-yes," I stuttered.

"Good! Good! Very good indeed!" Turning to his sister with a twinkle in his eye, he remarked that there appeared to be some hope for me at any rate, as I didn't appear to be colour blind!

"Come into my study next door. I'll check you out on the twelve times table first; then we'll go on to adding-ups, subtraction, and things like that. Knowing your grandfather Evan George, the master grocer of the Cwm, as I do, he's bound to ask if you've learned anything useful for your half crown, so I'll teach you all about simple interest before you go home. That ought to keep him happy, hey, what what?"

I started to take a liking to Uncle. Although I had a chronic dislike of maths, I decided to give it a go by concentrating like billy-o.

Scooting my heavy machine uphill past the Colliers Arms, Edna Grey's cottage, Jennie Sims's grocery shop, and Andrew Hopkins's fish and chip emporium was normally an exhausting experience, but repeating the simple interest formula all the way home made the trip somewhat easier

My tutor had told me not to attempt to remember SI = P x R x T over 100 for principal, rate, and time. Rather, when the subject of simple interest arose, I was to visualise a Cypriot who was over 100 years old! By spelling it as SIPRIOT over 100, I could easily recall the formula and arrive at the answer. Uncle was eccentric, all right—but I must confess to remembering that formula to this day, as I do many others that he taught me.

Uncle was also said to be quite rich by local standards, having invested money in metals in Canada and Australia. He was notably frugal. Rather than spend a penny on buying a newspaper, he would ride his bike—a 1903 French model with enormous wheels and solid tyres—three miles to the local public library at Peniel Green. There he could discover, free of charge in the reading room, the fortunes of his shares.

In our branch of the family, he was considered quite barmy, but loveable and useful.

———————◆◆◆◆——————

Some years after having been taught by Uncle, I began preparations to become a medical student. I was swatting one weekend when I was told that Sal, who drove one of the family bread vans, had been taken ill. I needed a break from wrestling with the intricacies of the prothalamion kephale in the brain of a dogfish, and I volunteered to attend to her delivery round.

It transpired that Uncle was one of her customers, purchasing a well-baked cob daily plus two batches at weekends. I duly arrived at his front door and found him kneeling by a second-hand replacement bike he'd purchased. Unlike his previous means of conveyance, it boasted pneumatic tyres, a bell, and mudguards. He was removing the front tyre, which was flat. Not having a repair outfit, he intended to withdraw the tube and fill the tyre with grass as a temporary measure. My arrival, it seemed, was timely.

First, I took care to say how sorry I was to have learned that his sister had passed away while I was at college. I then sought confirmation that he only wanted one cob. To my surprise, he asked for six brown loaves. Tearing off the crusts, he rolled them into thick, sausage-like shapes before stuffing them into the tyre and easing it over the rim of the wheel. The repair job was completed by firmly pushing a small rubber cork into the hole through which the tube valve would have protruded. I was informed that resorting to this trick had got him out of trouble several times over the past few months.

I was fascinated and enquired whether there was any particular significance in the colour of the bread, knowing brown bread to be more expensive. With a withering look, he said that brown bread was dense, like some people he knew, and therefore made firmer tyre packing!

As six loaves cost more than a puncture repair outfit, I felt pretty certain that a tube of solution, some patches, and a tin of talc would feature fairly high on his next shopping list.

The following day, a further calamity occurred. His chain had snapped, and he was waiting for me. "Ah! There you are, my dear chap! I was beginning to think you weren't coming. Be a good fellow and lend me your link extractor for a moment, will you?"

I had never seen or heard of a link extractor in my life. He seemed to think it rather odd that I didn't have one on me. Not wishing to be the recipient of another of those looks he reserved specifically for blithering idiots, I mumbled that I was sorry, but I had somehow mislaid it, and could I give him a lift somewhere?

Somewhat reluctantly, Uncle climbed into the van and asked if I was going anywhere near the library. I was obviously facing in another direction entirely, towards Birchgrove. As I prepared to turn round, he said that he had a confession to make—he had never ridden in a horseless bread van, or indeed any other motorised van before. He had a deep distrust bordering on fear of all types of machinery. He felt very much safer on a gun carriage or a horse. He was, he said, extremely suspicious of something propelled by a motive power that did not respond to instructions yelled to it, such as "gee up" or "wow". Further, he didn't like the look of the steering wheel and found it hard to believe that it was infinitely more precise than a pair of reins. In conclusion, he requested please would I remember to take it easy, and could he leave the door open so that he could make his escape should his fears be justified and the vehicle run out of control!

Though I never once got out of bottom gear all the way to Peniel Green, he was bordering on a nervous breakdown by the time I deposited him at his destination half an hour later. I doubt very much whether he made an intelligent appraisal of his riches that day.

The ride must have provided him with quite a thrill, however, because a week later, Sal, having recovered from the flu and got back on her round, called in at our house in Winchwen. She handed me a tiny threepenny bit with Queen Victoria's head on it, wrapped in a scrap of paper torn from an exercise book. On it, in exquisite copperplate writing, was the message, *For services rendered, And obliged H (MA London)*.

———————◆ ◆ ◆——————

The rear garden of Uncle's home had several fruit trees which were his pride and joy. Unfortunately, this orchard was frequently raided by children from the school in Church Road, who seemed to know instinctively when the apples and pears were ripe for plucking. Their attacks usually came at lunch hour.

Uncle received a useful sum from selling his crop to a lady who ran a grocery store across the street, sufficient—so he said anyway—to keep his bike in bread. This accorded fully with his maxim: "Charge for all your work and favours, and pay instantly for everything you receive, for this is the key respect." As he had never taken anything off anyone in his life without repaying in equal measure, he hated to be robbed.

One summer, his patience snapped after the kids made off with a particularly heavy haul while he was out on his bike. If he were the headmaster, he said (and here I might mention that George Bynon was my mother Doris's first cousin), he'd jolly well chain the bally lot to their desks at lunch hour.

Anticipating that his young arch-enemies would be back the next day, Uncle decided to give them the fright of their young lives—one that would ensure that they did not trouble him again.

Down in the cellar of his house was an old trunk which contained, along with a load of oriental bric-a-brac, his Indian Army dress uniform, a sword, and a rusty musket. Thus kitted out, he patiently lay in wait for the bandits to return on another raid. As they swarmed over the garden fence, he fired the musket in the air and charged down the path, holding his sword before him and yelling a blood-curdling Baluchi war cry.

The combination of the loud, unexpected bang and the sight of the military apparition descending rapidly upon them struck terror into the gang. In their haste to regain the road, they tried to climb over each other on their way up the fence, and fell back in a heap at Uncle's feet.

He commanded, "Hands up! Make a false move and I'll blow your heads off or rip you to bits for supper!" They willingly surrendered and allowed themselves to be marched around the side of the house onto the street. Uncle intended to take them to the police station for a wigging by the sergeant. However, the bang and subsequent round-up had not gone unobserved. Some of Uncle's neighbours phoned the vicar after a quick discussion, voicing fears that the old intellectual had gone irretrievably nuts.

One of the prisoners marched down the road with a pronounced limp. This set the phones ringing again, updating the vicar with the news that it looked as if Uncle had shot one of the children.

Things were beginning to sound serious, and the vicar contacted a local doctor. Halfway through the vicar's long-winded explanation, the doctor broke in to opine that it all seemed pretty harmless. On hearing of the shooting, he changed his mind, deciding it was a job for Sgt Dimmock. That was his initial verdict, anyway, as Uncle was using a double-barrelled musket and only one shot had yet been heard.

Without stopping for further explanation, these local powers disarmed and certified Uncle and arranged to have him sent to Cefn Coed, the town asylum, in a straitjacket. Here, when he got over the shock, Uncle took up the study of psychiatric medicine. In two years he had learned enough to prove to the authorities that he might be eccentric, but his sanity was unimpaired. He also got the principal doctor sacked for incompetence in the process.

When he returned to his home, he found that the vicar, the doctor, and the sergeant had all moved on, one way and another. His neighbours, feeling partly responsible for the torment he had undergone, had thoroughly cleaned and painted his house. But his lovely trees, which he had been looking forward to seeing laden, were denuded of fruit. They had succumbed to a succession of raids the week before, not only by his arch-enemies the schoolkids, but also by those who had been toiling to get his home straight.

The new village doctor was a much younger man than his predecessor. He called upon Uncle soon after his return. From what the doctor had heard, Uncle was by far the village's most colourful character, and he was longing to make his acquaintance. He wasn't disappointed. They became close friends, Uncle recognising the medic as a man of education and integrity like himself. The doctor felt, however, that Uncle was past being completely independent, and recommended that, while Uncle could continue to do his own washing, ironing, and other household chores, he really should have substantial meals made for him by someone else.

Uncle agreed to this suggestion, and was able shortly afterwards to inform the doctor that he had come to a suitable arrangement with Mrs Roberts. She was an almost destitute widow living opposite him, and agreed to make his daily meals, for which he would pay her fourteen shillings per week in advance.

There was one small problem, however. Mrs Roberts suffered from arthritis. Though this didn't affect her ability to make pies and things, the doctor thought that she should not be traipsing to and fro across the road every five minutes, fetching, carrying, and finding out what Uncle wanted to eat. Uncle understood. To save her the pain of this excessive exercise, and himself the sum of two bob, he hit on a novel method of informing her of his requirements. He also undertook to fetch the food from her kitchen himself, so long as he was well enough to do it. Subsequent weekly payments, of course, were reduced to twelve shillings!

To communicate with her, he tied a long piece of string across his bedroom window, from which he hung a variety of shaped and coloured pieces of cardboard. Each combination communicated a menu for the day. A red triangle with a blue oval, for instance, signified boiled beef and carrots followed by rice pudding. A black circle and a yellow square meant that he fancied bacon and egg with chips, along with crackers, gorgonzola cheese, and pickles.

To assist her in reading these orders, Mrs Roberts was supplied with Uncle's dead sister's opera glasses. After a few days of producing meals quite different from those ordered, she argued that she could see the signals better without it the glasses. Uncle refused to accept the logic of this. Upon investigation, it transpired that she had been looking through the wrong end!

———◆ ·· ◆———

One day, I received a message saying that Uncle wished to see me. Off I went to find out what it was all about.

After looking to the right and left of his front door to ensure that there was nobody in earshot, he told me that he wanted to get an important box out of Lloyds Bank in Morriston, and required a chauffeur-cum-bodyguard to go with him. He had thought of me because, as a relative and former pupil, I was one of the few people in the world that he trusted regarding his finances.

I informed him that I was keenly aware of this honour and would be around to pick him up in my father's Morris Eight at ten o'clock the following morning.

Well, we went the three miles to the bank. I was instructed to stand guard outside an office door while he and the manager conducted their business for twenty minutes or so. Eventually, Uncle popped his head out. He enquired conspiratorially if the coast was clear, and I assured him that there wasn't a shifty customer in sight. He then emerged carrying a steel box, instructing me to stay close to him in case he was attacked.

Reaching the street, we walked briskly to the car. Uncle got into the back with his precious cargo and told me to drive home flat out. At every street intersection, I watched fearfully. I expected at any moment to find a number of cars blocking me in and disgorging tough guys armed with weapons, Al Capone style! Fortunately, nothing of the sort occurred, and we eventually arrived outside Uncle's front door.

I stood guard over the car while Uncle proceeded to check his home from top to bottom for intruders. When he was satisfied that there no one lay in wait for him and his precious box, I carried it into his lounge and set it down in the middle of the floor. Uncle double-bolted his front door. I acceded to his request to draw the curtains tight shut, wondering if I would be entrusted with a view of the riches the box contained. I fully expected to be asked to leave the room for a few moments.

Instead, Uncle told me to guard the box with my life while he went to get its key from an old safe under his staircase. Shortly, he was back. I held my breath as he knelt down and opened the robust lock.

Nonchalantly flipping back the hasp, he slowly lifted the lid, looking up at me with an enormous grin on his face as he did. I couldn't believe my eyes. Instead of the bags of coins, trays of gems, and wads of notes I was expecting to see, the box only contained an old copy of the *Evening Post*. Horror-stricken, I spluttered that it was empty and sought an explanation for his apparent unconcern.

"Ah!" he said. "I didn't want to tell you beforehand that we were only going on a dry run, as you might not have been sufficiently vigilant. But now that I've put you to the test and found what a good bodyguard you are, I will have no hesitation whatsoever in calling on your assistance should I ever wish to remove a full box from Lloyds Bank in future!"

That's when I decided that there really might be something in the family's private belief that Uncle was actually off his head and should have remained in the nuthouse.

———————◆ ◆ ◆———————

A year later, my mother and father were awakened about six o'clock one morning by a loud knocking on their back door. They were surprised to see Uncle. They asked where he was going at that time of the morning and were informed that he was off to America in the *Queen Mary*, and could Father lend him a shilling? Sensibly, Father mentioned that he thought the trip would cost rather more than that, but was told that the shilling was to post a parcel from Southampton to Uncle's solicitor.

He was invited to join them for breakfast. As Mother lit the fire and prepared the table, Uncle told Father that he had decided to leave the bulk of his fortune to his nephew in the States. Not trusting the overseas post in this respect (he recollected sending several letters from the Punjab many years before that had not arrived home), he felt it was much safer to go over and tell the chap personally. He would also have the opportunity of meeting and judging him. He had already written to say he was coming, though he had been careful not to say why. His nephew had replied that Uncle would be most welcome in his humble home, and the family looked forward to meeting him.

In order to make the trip economically, Uncle had asked for a cabin down near the bilges. "After all," he pointed out, "it's only to sleep in, and I only sleep four hours a day." Frankly, I wouldn't have been surprised if he'd asked for a price reduction on this score.

Mother asked where his luggage was. Uncle explained that he had rolled up some shirts and collars in his overcoat pockets. The pockets of his jackets held handkerchiefs and a packet of herring sandwiches. He also informed her that he was wearing three pairs of combinations, recalling how some of the survivors of the RMS *Titanic* had mentioned how cold it was on the deck after they struck the iceberg.

Uncle proposed to cycle to Southampton and sell his bike on arrival. He had arranged with the Cunard Line, which operated the ship, to give lectures in Russian and Urdu during the trip, for which he was to be paid. He left our house around seven o'clock that morning, handing

Father an IOU for a shilling written on the back of a bus ticket, and promising to honour it as soon as he got back.

Such was his success on the ship that Cunard asked him to repeat the lessons on the return journey—but I'm jumping ahead of events a little.

It seems Uncle got to New York City and was promptly run over by a cab while searching for his nephew. He was carted off to hospital for repairs—an expensive business which more or less absorbed his Cunard teaching fees. His nephew found him a few days later, and, being sufficiently recovered to travel, Uncle was whisked off in an enormous chauffeur-driven Cadillac limousine to a huge ranch—one of the nephew's three holiday retreats in upper New York State.

Uncle had not at this time explained the purpose of his visit. Having seen his nephew's twelve-room home, embellished with interior and exterior swimming pools, games room, tennis court, cattle and horses, and so on, and having established that this was only a part of the nephew's wealth as an executive vice president of one of America's largest steel conglomerates, the Bethlehem Steel Corporation, Uncle concluded that what he had proposed to leave his nephew would only amount to a couple of months' pocket money. Under the circumstances, Uncle felt that he could find better use for the bequest—like building an extension onto the local library in memory of his sister and refurbishing the clock on Llansamlet parish church.

So Uncle enjoyed the hospitality of his American relative for three weeks. He regaled the family with tales of Wales and the ancestors his brother had told his children about. Then, not wishing to outstay his welcome, he caught the

Queen Mary back to Southampton, making up some of his financial losses along the way by offering morning classes in English literature and in Welsh.

On arrival in the great port, he chanced to see the porter to whom he had sold his bike. This worthy complained bitterly that he had only been able to use it for a few days before it sustained a terminal gash in one of its tyres. As the wheel size was different to that on modern machines, it was impossible to find a replacement tyre in Southampton. As far as the porter was concerned, the bike was now no more than a heap of junk.

Uncle, who had a spare tube and tyre in his loft at home, immediately offered to buy it back at half price. The porter, delighted that his bargain wasn't going to be a complete financial disaster, went to fetch it from a nearby shed. Uncle handed over three shillings and promptly pushed the machine into the centre of the city, where he boarded the train for Swansea.

Eventually, Uncle arrived on our doorstep, but at a much more respectable hour than previously. Having imparted every detail of his trip to Mother over tea and scones, he asked for the return of his IOU in exchange for some money, saying that he hoped Father wouldn't mind repayment in dimes!

———————◄ ◄ ► ►———————

I was in the Llansamlet greengrocer's one day with my fiancée Marion when I spotted Uncle propping up his bike against the curb outside She'd heard all about him, of course, and I introduced them when he entered.

Uncle's dress, while impeccable, was some sixty years behind the times. His starched collar was curved, his cap had a prominent button on top, and the peak was spanned by a thin leather belt. His breeches terminated in long woollen hose, and his feet were shod in brown leather boots which were mirror shiny. In addition, Uncle sported a Harris tweed jacket secured by six leather buttons, the generously flapped pockets being secured in a like manner.

Marion stared at him, fascinated. He took her hand gently in his and told her in a deep, cultured voice how delighted he was to make her acquaintance. She was hooked, and readily accepted his offer to treat us to tea the following afternoon.

We arrived promptly at four o'clock and were ushered into his dining room, where we were handed glasses of gooseberry wine. Uncle informed Marion that he knew some of her relatives who were of his age, and also revealed that he had discovered a connection between the two families. Not wanting to miss the slightest scrap of information, she followed the old man back and forth, carrying plates of food from the kitchen to the table. The two seemed to get on together as though they had been pals for years.

If Uncle's information was sound, then one of Marion's great-aunties had eloped with my great-grandfather's third cousin Trevor to Patagonia, which was just about as far as one could run from home. There, they had become prosperous ranchers and had brought up a brood of eleven children, some of whom had subsequently turned up in the village while on European tours.

Uncle recalled one group arriving who didn't know a scrap of the English language. They only spoke Welsh and

Spanish, and their Welsh was of a purity seldom heard in Wales today outside of a pulpit on Sundays. It seems this was because the only book Aunty and Trevor took with them was a Welsh Bible. It had served to teach their children (and many others in their neighbourhood) everything from grammar to literature to history to geography—not counting, of course, religion. As Aunty was articulate and fairly well educated, she had been asked to undertake service as district teacher, which she apparently took in her stride, even though the nearest bookshop had been hundreds of miles away in Buenos Aires. She eventually became the district education superintendent.

Uncle suggested that, should either or both of us go out that way—and he made it sound as if this could be accomplished any old weekend—we could look up Aunty and Trevor in the graveyard in Cormoro Rivadavia, about halfway down the eastern coastline of Argentina. Marion told me later that she had almost expected Uncle to say that they'd be delighted to see us!

Uncle's festive tea table had been adorned with a beautifully crocheted cloth. Uncle produced a superb Royal Doulton Peaches tea set of the finest bone china from a cupboard which appeared to be crammed with the exquisite stuff.

Unlike in Japan, my old tutor's tea-making ceremony was not a joy to behold. A more apt description would be "excruciatingly interesting". As there were three of us, he commenced by measuring three and a quarter cups of rainwater from a barrel outside his back door into a small kettle, explaining as he did so that he had always avoided tap water like the plague for fear of lead poisoning.

The ceremony was a lesson in economy. He rightly pointed out that a small kettle required less heat to warm than a large one, and that it was a waste to put in more water than required However, it was necessary to put in an additional quarter cup to allow for evaporation. Should any water happen to be left over, it could be returned to the barrel.

As we sat down to tea, my fiancée noticed that the solid silver knives, forks, and spoons were greenish in colour. Uncle, smiling at her obvious concern, explained that it was folly to rub silver too frequently. Being a noble metal and relatively soft, some of its value might be lost.

We were treated to Welsh cakes and teishen lap for eats. Halfway through the meal and an animated conversation, Uncle realised that he hadn't changed the colour-coded signals in his bedroom window. He feared that Mrs Roberts would repeat his luncheon order for supper. Apologising profusely, he left us and went upstairs like a shot to replace the green square and black triangle (fish and chips) for a brown circle and a white oblong (casserole with jelly and cream).

On his return, we were informed that he had only the previous week pushed his bike, laden with cans of paint and a ladder, some six miles or so to Eaton Crescent the other side of our town and back—no mean feat for a man of eighty. We enquired what could possibly have inspired this marathon, as neither Marion nor I could imagine him going into the painting and decorating business at his age.

Laughing, he told us he had a large property there which he had rented out for many years. Apparently, the tenants had complained that part of the conservatory on the side of the building was on the point of collapse and posed a danger. So Uncle had arranged with a builder to remove the offending part and make good what was left. It had occurred to Uncle, while inspecting the work, that the frontage of the building was now some seventeen inches shorter and therefore might qualify for a reduction in the rates. A letter from the corporation confirmed the fact and informed him that he would owe six shillings less per year in future. Uncle spent this six shillings on paint, a brush, and white spirits, and painted the repaired conservatory himself after establishing that the builder proposed to charge him six shillings and ninepence for the work!

My last contact with Uncle was when he was 84 years old. A colleague who had been with him at the League of Nations passed away, and a letter to this effect arrived at the local post office for distribution by the postman. The postmistress noticed that the envelope had "Urgent" written across the top. As her husband the postman wasn't due back from his first round for another hour or so, she asked me if I would be kind enough to deliver it. I agreed.

As usual, Uncle was glad to see me and thanked me for bringing the mail. He took the letter and began a lengthy search of his numerous pockets for his glasses. He then meticulously cleaned them with a piece of paper ripped from the *Evening Post*, explaining as he did so that there was no finer medium to be found for cleaning glass. He followed with an involved explanation of why he thought that this was true, remarking that not all newsprint was of the same quality. He thought that the degree of moisture in the paper and the type of pulp had something to do with it.

Before we got botanically bogged down, I reminded him of the urgency of the communication. He scrutinised the envelope keenly, noting disapprovingly that there was no sender's name and address on the back.

The next three or four minutes were taken up in searching for an envelope slitter, which he was sure he had returned to his bureau after making holes with it in the lid of a jam jar. As it looked as though the required article wasn't coming to light, I suggested that a knife or other implement would do the job for him. He reluctantly prised the letter open with a chisel.

I have to admit I was curious and thought I would now discover the nature of the urgency. But Uncle wasn't finished yet. Withdrawing the contents of the envelope, he proceeded to count the number of sheets and then started to read out aloud.

When he got to the date, he paused to get a pencil, which he sharpened to a very fine point. Next he made an alteration, as he thought that the date should be "3/7/48" and not "July 3rd '48", as written. This resulted in the date becoming almost unintelligible. A further ransacking of his bureau was called for in order to find a rubber.

I was on the point of pulling my hair out, but was thankfully prevented from doing so by Uncle's condescending to proceed. "My dear H," he read, and paused again to correct a spelling mistake in his name.

"With much regret," he continued, "I have to inform you of—" Further pause to change this to "I regret to have to inform you of".

"—the passing of our old comrade." ("Good heavens!" said Uncle in an agitated aside. "Pasqual Rodriguez seems to have gone bolshy!" He crossed out "comrade" and substituted "colleague", then read from the start once again. "Ah! That's a lot better!")

So it went on to the bitter end, with Uncle reading the letter from the beginning each time a correction was made. By the time he had finished, he was badly in need of a new pencil and rubber. I expected him to express surprise or sorrow or something at the news that his co-worker had departed this life after being attacked and devoured by wolves in the Arctic, but all he said was that Pasqual Rodriguez never had mastered the English language properly, for all his schooling!

I had accepted a temporary job at this time, working three counties away, and I felt most strongly that the job was my salvation. Any further association with Uncle would most likely have left me pretty close to bonkers myself, which wouldn't have made my new missus very happy.

2

Tangling with Imperial Fuzz

In the United Kingdom in 1956, we were to tangle hilariously with the police on more than one occasion. It should be explained that the number plates "FIFI" on our car were something of a novelty there, though quite normal in South Arabia. Each plate was painted with a black background and a thick yellow border. There were English letters and numbers in white on the left side, and Arabic letters and numbers on the right, separated from one another by a bright red flower. Such flowers (there were a number of types and colours at the source) were not embellishments, but rather served to assist those policemen who couldn't read to pin vehicles down to a locality.

Tangle Number One

We were parked outside Woolworth's in mid-Oxford Street in our home town one Saturday afternoon, at a spot with a twenty-minute time restriction. The Mem had already been gone an hour. I was a bit apprehensive over the two policemen about to walk past me for the third time.

I looked elsewhere yet again, pretending not to know they were there, but this time to no avail. In my mirror, I saw them make directly for me, and I opened the window, trying to look a lot happier than I felt.

"Good morning, sir," said the older of the two. "Speak English, do you?"

"Yes indeed, officer. And Welsh too!"

This bit of boasting was obviously a mistake, as he reached for his notebook. He knew I was well over time, but would have forgiven me quite readily, I think, if I had turned out to be a foreigner.

"Where are you from?" asked the younger officer.

"Llansamlet," I replied truthfully. "But I actually work in Aden."

"Driven all the way then, have you?" He obviously didn't have a clue where Aden was, except that he was certain that it wasn't in Wales.

Fleetingly, I imagined what might be going on in his head in the taffy English of Swansea: "Played rugby all over the motherland, I 'ave. That's all over the land of my fathers, like, see. And I would shoely 'ave 'eard of the place. Can't be very important if it don't 'ave a team, though."

"Yes, all the way," I lied. "Long trip too, I can tell you!"

"Right, then," interrupted the older man, licking the tip of his pencil. "Let's see what we got. One: parking in the main street for nearly an hour. Two: telling lies to the police, i.e., stating that your car 'ave swum the Channel!"

I winced, as it was beginning to sound expensive.

He smiled, and a strange, faraway look crept into his eyes. "Well, well! Fancy meeting a bloke what's come all the way from Aden, then! Of course, man, I should have recognised them plates with the old flowers, isn't it? Posted there once, I was. Deuce, there's a hell of a place for squaddies! In the SWABs[1] I was, see. There was this damn big plaque of our outfit up the top of the Aqaba, at the entrance to Crater.[2] It was right opposite a police station. 'The 24th Regiment of Foot', it said, and above it was a picture of the Sphinx. 'Pharaoh's pooch', we used to call it! Had to paint the bloody thing on jankers once, I did. It put me and my mates in the RAF hospital up Tarshyne for weeks. Nearly burned to a frazzle, we was. Er, still there, I suppose, is it?"

I assured him it was. "Tell me, were you ever up in Dering Lines in Brecon?" I asked hopefully.

"I'm sorry, I don't know what you're talking about, sir," said the young cop.

"Hush, lad," murmured his colleague. "Still talking to me, the gentleman is." He stared at me closer still, wondering, I suppose, whether he might have seen me before. "Know the Lines then, do you? I used to be a drill sergeant up by there, man."

---

[1] South Wales Borderers Regiment.
[2] Capital city of Aden Colony.

"Oh, I know the Lines and the barracks well. Did my primary training up in Brecon with the SWABs," I replied. "Our squad billet had the name Blenheim over the door."

"Ay, boy! Of course I knew Blenheim. Dug the lads out of there many a morning, I can tell you, and straight up to the range at Cwm Gwdi with them, full pack and rifle and all! Yes, Blenheim! Bloody old Nissen hut it was, remember?"

"Not likely to forget in a hurry, Sergeant," I replied, addressing him by his old army rank. "I suppose you must have known my old drill sergeant—a bloke called McKinlly? Damned near broke my heart those first six weeks, did McKinlly, but I must say that I was grateful to him later on. I hated his guts at the time, but I do admit, he make a man of me!"

"So old McKinlly was your instructor, was he? Well, well! Big mates, McKinlly and me, indeed. We was always competing to see whose squad could get the most first-class certificates of training. Mind you, McKinlly was a tough old bugger, I can tell you. Made all his men learn the 'istory of the regiment by 'eart, he did.

"Do you know, I can hear 'im shouting now, man. 'Hey you! Yes, you next to the marker. How many Victoria Crosses did we win when we was fighting the Fuzzie Wuzzies in South Africa then?' The lad barked out the right answer to 'im, see. 'Quite right. Good boy,' McKinnly replied, 'and don't forget it was before breakfast too, mind you. Now then, you over there. Third man in the centre rank. How many Fuzzies did we shoot and bayonet? Come on, boy! Out with it quick! *Don't know, sergeant*? What the 'ell do you mean, you don't know? What would your mother think if she 'eard you by here now, then? It's disgusting to think of. Never make a good SWAB, you. Worse than that, boy, you wouldn't even make the Hedication Corps! Now pay attention careful-like, in case the commandin' hofficer do ask you. It was two thousand shot and a hundred and forty eight point six bayoneted. Got it?' Deuce, man. Great on 'istory was old McKinlly, indeed!"

The younger man now adopted the sort of look one often saw on the faces of those who had either missed or dodged military service and were obliged to listen to the adventures of veterans. I can't explain that look, but I know it well, and so, perhaps, may you.

The older officer suddenly came back to the present. "Look! We haven't seen you, OK? Now push off, there's a good lad."

"Any idea where I can park legally for another twenty minutes?" I asked, feeling sure the Mem must be getting danger vibes by now.

"I suppose you could park by here," said the older policeman thoughtfully. "It should be all right."

"Pardon? How come, then?" I asked, a bit confused.

"Well, if you are not by here when I am here, I can't book you, see? And if you go round the block and find when you come back that there I am, gone, I still won't be able to book you, right? So what are you waiting for, man?"

"Er, right!" I agreed, certain that there was perfect reasoning somewhere in that piece of froth. "OK then! Thank you. Thank you very much. See you!"

Saluting, the two officers moved off, and so did I—to the car park. With my kind of luck, they would surely have had a shift change or something, and the chances of

27

bumping into two SWABs in one day, I felt, was pretty remote.

Adrenalin heightens all sorts of powers, and in my imagination, I was still tuned in to the conversation of the two cops. The younger policeman was puzzled. "Why didn't you book 'im?" he asked

"Ah! Well, that is where experience comes in, see, lad. Hofficers of the law do 'ave a lot of power, as they no doubt taught you in the police college up Cwmbran, and they've got to use it wisely, like. There is such a thing as discretion, isn't it?"

"Aye!" muttered the youngster under his breath. "And there is such a thing as the old regimental tie too, and I think I just seen it working!"

Tangle Number Two

Less than a week after the first encounter with my home-town constabulary, I had another narrow escape. The powers that be had decided, while I was out of the country, to make the lane behind Davy's taxi garage a one-way street. Not only that, but they also placed a police box there. I expect you've guessed it—a constable was just coming out of it as I was passing, travelling in the wrong direction!

I suppose I could have carried straight on in the hope that he wouldn't be able to make much of Fifi's number plates. On the other hand, once seen, never forgotten, as they say, and we would be around the town for another month. So I stopped and waited for him to catch up.

He strode purposefully towards me, taking in Fifi's interesting rear as he came. He'd been good at Kim's Game in the scouts, and noticed that the offender was an odd-looking Ford with wings and things. There was a funny number plate on it, upon which somebody appeared to have scrawled in white paint. "And bless me if it didn't have a flower in the middle!" He also took in an international plate with ADN on it, which didn't register with him. He did note that the vehicle had right-hand drive. As far as he was aware, the only other country where they drove on the right side was Japan. But the fellow in the car looked more brown than yellow. He couldn't see the driver's eyes, however, as they were hidden behind reflective glasses.

The constable decided to be nice, even though his uncle Bill had been in one of their prison camps. "Hello!" he greeted me. "You speekee Eengeeleesh?"

The devil was in me. Nodding my head vigorously, I replied, "Si a velli, small peess. Much tiny leetl, I theenk!"

"Ah! Velee good." He beamed. Then, pointing a finger imperiously, he continued, "Thees one-way streetee. Up by there, no go. Down back way, okay. See?" He was pointing his finger in so many directions that I found it quite painful to nod and turn my head all over the place at the same time.

As is almost inevitable on such occasions, a small crowd had gathered—eager to see the outcome, and ready to tut-tut to a man if I was booked. The officer turned towards them, seeking their approval at this obvious demonstration of police skills. I, momentarily elevating my specs, winked furiously at them from behind him.

"Lookee, lookee," he continued, turning back to me. "When me go stopee car, car, you come backee down, down, chop, chop. Then me say you goodee bye, bye, cheerio. Savvy?"

He walked smartly into the centre of Wind Street and waved a Number 76 double-decker from Port Tennant to a halt. I gave the crowd a thumbs-up sign. Feeling as though my head would fall off at any moment, I slowly backed up to the junction. The throng, meanwhile, were enjoying the situation and had begun to clap and cheer a bit.

The policeman was feeling quite proud of himself. He had just completed a community communications course where they'd taught him a thing or two about how to make friends and influence people. He'd passed second from the top. The reactions of these happy people provided him with ample evidence that he'd really learned his stuff and that it worked.

While his efforts were commendable, this was not quite the case, however. The truth was that the crowd were aware of something that had all the time been obscured from the bobby's view—namely, Fifi's radiator grill. You see, thereon were prominently displayed two badges, one having a beautiful dragon with the word "Cymru" (Wales) underneath it, and the other proclaiming the owner to be a member of the Swansea Motoring Club!

Tangle Number Three

Our final brush with the forces of "Loran D'Order" in Britain occurred on the very day we were returning overseas. It happened near Henley-on-Thames. We were taking Fifi to a large company in London which, among other things, could give her a thorough overhaul and then have her shipped to us. The Mem and I meanwhile flew out of Heathrow on a Britannia affectionately known as the "Whispering Giant".

Heavily laden with baggage though she was, Fifi could still move quite rapidly, and I gave her her head. I was sitting back, enjoying the thrill of it all, imagining I was Fangio, when a sleek Bristol saloon went by making me feel as though we were motoring backwards.

"He's doing over a ton, isn't he, darling?" enquired a disapproving Mem.

"You bet he is!" I replied, green with envy. "And did you notice the nonchalant way he was lighting a cigarette as he passed us?"

The police Jaguar seemed to appear from nowhere about two minutes later. I'm normally a great one for watching what's happening astern of me through the mirror, but I somehow missed this chap's arrival on my tail. I pulled in slightly to let him go, but he merely flashed his headlights, illuminated his police sign, and played a few bars of some obscure music on his siren. It dawned on me then that we were his customers. Putting on our left winker, in case he thought we might be harbouring any thoughts about accelerating to Fifi's full potential and leaving him on the horizon, I slowed down and pulled into a lay-by a hundred yards or so further on.

"Our luck's playing up again, honey," I warned the Mem.

Here came a sergeant and a constable. "Good morning, sir."

"Er, good morning. Look, I had no idea we were going quite so fast!"

"Oh! Were you, sir? I must confess that we hadn't really noticed. Would you mind getting out of the car and opening the boot, please?"

I hastened to do as I was told, and asked what the problem was. They told me that a dangerous prisoner had escaped from a local prison and, when last seen, was being assisted into the boot of a car the colour of ours. "Not much room for him in yours, though, sir. Not with all that baggage!"

I laughed with relief and told them that we hadn't stopped all the way from South Wales. "Right, then. Can we go now?" I asked.

"While we're at it, can I see your green card, sir? And show me what sort of licence you're using."

The Mem fished out the card and my international licence from her commodious bag, and the sergeant studied them carefully. "How long have you been in UK, sir?"

"Four months," I replied—quite wrongly, of course. That had been my leave period, and much of it had been spent on the ship coming home and in driving through Europe. I really should have told him three.

"In that case, sir, I have to point out that you've committed an offence. If you stay more than ninety days, you have to take out British taxation." At least, that's what I understood him to say.

I immediately got on my high horse, a silly thing to do with the fuzz. "I haven't actually used it here for ninety days," I protested. "It was in the garage all the time we were visiting Ireland. Anyway, look here, I'm ruddy well fed up with the way you people treat us every time we venture on the road in this country. We've been travelling all over the Middle East and Europe, and we haven't had a minute's trouble from the police anywhere else. What's wrong with this damned place? I've got a good mind to complain to my MP!"

The two officers looked gravely at each other, then back at me. I could tell they were wondering if I was threatening them.

"Yes? And who might your MP be?" enquired the sergeant.

"Abdul Shareef al Awal," I replied seriously. "And I don't think he'll like it one little bit, I can tell you!"

"And this is your last day in the country, sir, is that right?"

"That's right," I said. "And it would be just my rotten luck to miss the plane over something like this!"

"Yes, that's the way things go," he commiserated. "Look, do you mind moving on, sir? Or we'll be nicking you for impeding officers of the law in the course of their duty—like catching real criminals!"

I looked at him, somewhat surprised, as I'd expected him to be difficult.

"Abdul Shoofti Awal, indeed!" He chuckled. "Ten out of ten for effort, sir!" Giving Fifi a friendly pat on the roof, he dashed back to the Jag with his driver and roared off in pursuit of an apple-green Mini.

"Phew! That was a close one," I said to the Mem.

"Er, yes, darling But the criminal can't be all that dangerous," she observed. "They must have been exaggerating a teeny bit, don't you think? I mean, you couldn't pack a dwarf easily into the boot of that Riley Elf!"

"That's right, honey," I replied, easing Fifi out of the lay-by. "Well, not if it's carrying a spanner or two as well!"

3

The East Side
Home Guard

My father went to a midweek meeting in 1940 in our chapel hall. It wasn't a prayer meeting or anything like that. It was to discuss the feasibility of forming a military unit to protect the eastern approaches of our valley from the Germans.

Groups of old warriors, supplemented by potential young warriors who were unfit for service in the principal armed forces, had been formed all over the country under the initial title of "local defence volunteers". Armed with double-barrel shotguns, pitchforks, and similar weapons of varying ferocity, these volunteers were to be seen practising their drills on village greens and town and city squares, wearing macs, waistcoats, trilbys, and cloth caps A white band with the letters LDV on it was worn on the left arm to show who they were.

The name was quickly changed to the Home Guard, and uniforms were provided as soon as available—a sensible move, as the Nazis might otherwise have executed them all if captured.

There was no shortage of volunteers, and they were led by officers and NCOs who had seen service in the Great War and knew their stuff, even though they were getting a bit stiff in the limbs. Some of these acquired a new and respectable status overnight and absolutely revelled in it all.

Well, a unit was formed in our place shortly afterwards. Without exception, they were all good, honest, God-fearing men, prepared to defend their own ground and loved ones tooth and nail—there being very few other weapons available at the time. Initially, however, there was a problem. None of the "old sweats" in our village had been an officer, and it was felt that there ought to be one. They looked among themselves for the man best qualified.

Thomas Hopkyn was the chief clerk at the local steel works. He was a deacon in the chapel and a gentleman as well; he owned six houses in the village. Not only had he gone up the ladder of success, but he had also once been to India by sea as a fare-paying passenger, travelling posh there and back.

Here was the obvious choice for platoon lieutenant, and it mattered little to the men that the only weapon he had ever wielded in anger was a pencil sharpener. He also had one other attribute which everyone thought might come in handy: he could pray better than anybody else in the village except the Reverend Lloyd Jones!

The NCOs got cracking right away. Though unable to get their men quite up to Brigade of Guards standard, they were certain that they would all give a pretty good account of themselves, arthritis and flat feet permitting. To test their mettle, a secret exercise was planned.

They were informed that one weekend, they would be involved in stopping "the enemy" from getting at the factories and pits that proliferated in the valley. This enemy would come ashore at the docks of a nearby town, and if they succeeded in their mission, the nation would be severely disabled. With their fearsome Backa-Bombard, Lewis gun, and ten rifles (ex. Somme, Ypres, Rouke's Drift, and Canada), and their pitchforks sharpened to needle points, the guardsmen were determined that nothing was going to get through on the eastern approach to the valley while any of them remained alive.

Trenches were dug in several favourable locations, and many old bones had creaked through the filling of dozens of sandbags. The most popular trench was the one they dug at the rear of Dai Jenkins's fish and chip shop. This commanded a superb view of the valley and its approaches. It was an excellent location for the supply of fags, victuals, and drinks. And the heavy Backa-Bombard and its ammunition could be kept under lock and key in the shed next to Jenkins's coalhouse. From there, it could be got into action fast without the troops getting pooped carrying it.

They waited several weekends for the Nazi hordes or other enemy to come, but nothing happened. Either the War Office didn't have enough enemy forces to spare, or they preferred not to say when they were coming. Even more likely, the Nazis had heard on the grapevine that there were about two million Home Guards in the country besides the regular troops, and were hesitating because they were scared stiff.

As time went on, the tension relaxed. Not only did some of the men put their weapons on the floor for a bit of a rest, but Lieutenant Hopkyn started to let a few at a time go home to lunch. This was not considered too risky, as most of the Home Guards lived no more than fifteen minutes from the chip shop. Those who weren't deaf would easily hear the lieutenant's whistle if they were needed quickly.

Shortly afterwards, fate took a hand at an inopportune moment. It was often suggested, in hindsight, that there might have been a quisling in the village.

The time had come around for the annual big meetings in chapel. Though it was not absolutely imperative for Lieutenant Hopkyn to be there, occupying his place in the big seat below the pulpit with the other deacons, it was also unheard of for any Hopkyn in the past five generations not to be present on such an important occasion.

So, taking what those in higher military circles call a "calculated risk", the lieutenant went. He could not be said to be AWOL (absent without leave), as he was actually the local military boss. And he had arranged to place the trenches, men, and weapons in the capable hands of Sgt Powell. Sgt Powell had been selected not because he was more experienced than the other sergeants in the platoon, but because he could see further down the valley without glasses.

To demonstrate the power vested in him by his superior officer, and to court popularity with the other ranks (given that there was the prospect of promotion to sergeant major), Sgt Powell doubled the number of blokes allowed to go home for refreshments. This, of course, halved the number of guardsmen available to oppose any attack.

The sergeant looked long and hard down the valley for any signs of alien activity, but all was calm. There was just the usual rail traffic between the docks and the factories, and some shunting of waggons in the sidings below the chip shop. Still, as his platoon was now a bit thin on the ground, so to speak, he thought it prudent to order, "Fix bayonets!"

A long train of waggons and carriages was being hauled towards them from the Upper Bank main station in Pentre, the next village down. It was probably bringing a further load of food, tanks, and equipment from America. Above, lethal aircraft left white trails in the cloudless sky.

Back at the chapel, the service finished and everybody filed out Lieutenant Hopkyn was the deacon responsible for changing the hymn number cards on the boards on either side of the organ. In this capacity, he went into the little room at the back to get the numbers for the evening service. He therefore missed the drama of the congregation being rounded up outside the graveyard by a group of soldiers of the Scottish Black Watch Regiment, who had got off the train in an embankment out of sight of the trenches.

The soldiers' faces were blackened with boot polish, and tufts of grass were stuffed into the netting on their helmets They spoke a strange form of English and were assumed to be colonial troops, but obviously ours. Accordingly, on being asked, the villagers had no hesitation in pinpointing the exact location of the local Home Guard unit. You see, the villagers were not privy to the fact that an exercise was expected, as that was top secret.

Keeping a very low profile behind them, the Black Watch herded the bewildered villagers towards the chip shop, making them sing a popular Welsh hymn as they went.

Sgt Powell and the chaps in the trenches thought it a bit strange that all the congregation were walking together the same way from chapel and singing "Wele Cawsom y Messiah"—lovely too—but they concluded that the lieutenant had arranged for them not to miss all the big meeting by bringing some of it to the front line, so to speak. The sergeant knew his duty in such circumstances.

"Right, lads! Smarten up there! You can see who is coming towards you. Keep a sharp lookout down the valley, now. It's your nearest and dearest what will be watching you, mind."

Their nearest and dearest were almost upon them when the congregation came to the amen at the end of the hymn, led by Llew "Top Note" and his famous tremolo double C.

The guardsmen were squinting hard over their rifle sights and singing along with their families when the Black Watch suddenly pounced, taking them prisoner. Our heroes were all rounded up and locked in the peeling and chipping room of Jenkins's premises—watched carefully by a soldier with a skirt on, shame to say!

The congregation was sent home, and the Black Watch moved on to test the mettle of the next lot of Home Guards. These were defending the valley's stock of ale at the Llanofni Inn, a mile and a half up the road.

As it would have been unseemly to fire Lieutenant Hopkyn, a longstanding pillar of the community, torn as he was between his duty to his Maker and his fellow men, the War Office promoted him to captain, out of harm's way.

Seventy years young, Lieutenant General Sir Martin Probarts, KCB, KSI, DSO, MC, had recently come to reside with his nephew, the vicar. He was now approached up at the manor house and asked if he fancied taking on the important job of lieutenant of the village platoon. Being a type of lieutenant himself, it was felt that he would be a natural for the task. Sir Martin was delighted to be called again to serve king and country after having done so faithfully and well up the Khyber, at Kimberley, in Egypt, and in Flanders fields. He came down to the chip shop like a shot, his moustaches waxed to perfection and fresh creases in his plus fours. To resounding cheers from the guardsmen, his butler wheeled him in in his bath chair to take command.

Sir Martin Probarts must have been the only lieutenant in the British army with red tabs on his collar and the experience of a corps commander behind him. But what was more important was the fact that he had brought his 1914 military-issue binoculars with him, thus trebling the observational powers of the unit. Further, in case these got lost or damaged in action, the unit could call on a somewhat less powerful backup, Sir Martin having access to Lady Girtie Probarts' opera glasses.

As she didn't like the idea of anyone else handling them, she insisted on coming down to the chip shop herself. She was often to be seen sitting behind the Backa-Bombard in a deck chair, knitting socks and balaclava helmets for the troops, the vital glasses residing on her ample bosom. From time to time, she would put down her needles and wool and relieve Sgt Powell by doing a bit of "shoofti work" herself, as she was wont to call it. Other times, she would massage Sir Martin's gouty toes or dispense lettuce and potato sandwiches to the lads, along with bottles of her elderberry wine.

Naturally, none of this went down very well with Jenkins at the chip shop, who was heard grumbling that the ruddy landed gentry were robbing him of his bread and butter.

With such a distinguished military leader directing operations behind the Backa-Bombard, local morale was very high. The guardsmen boasted that the War Office could send as many Black Watchmen as they liked—or, for that matter, any other damned colour they had in stock. Next time, there was no way they would get past 114 Platoon, Glamorganshire Home Guard, leave alone eat the Llanofni Inn out of house and home. They or the Nazi army would be buried right here in the trenches behind the chip shop!

Well, the platoon remained supremely alert for the next four years, but the enemy never came—not from either side.

Postscript

Towards the end of 1944, Colonel Hopkyn, MBE, came to take the salute and congratulate them on their disbandment parade. He mentioned how proud he was to have once had the honour of commanding them. The 114th proudly marched past him as he stood on the saluting dais. Lieutenant General Sir Martin Probarts, KCB, KSI, KIE, DSO, MC, was at their head, his wheelchair newly painted sky blue after having been in dowdy green-and-khaki camouflage for so long.

Bringing up the rear, on a milk cart pulled by Mrs Bevan's old horse, Dobbin, and urged along by Sgt Major Powell cracking a whip importantly, was the weapon around which their lives had revolved for much of the war. The Backa-Bombard too, had been given a new coat of paint—though it didn't look half as menacing in a delicate shade of pink!

4

Ah, There You Are—Er, Um ...

When you're a bit of a know-it-all, a salutary experience is to watch that TV programme in which awfully clever people have to sit in a chair and answer a barrage of questions on their chosen subject, chucked at them by that chap from Iceland—or is it Greenland? Can't recall his name for the moment, or the name of the programme for that matter. Of course, they've all got memories like sponges.

I developed mine many years ago, you know This chap persuaded me to purchase a course called "Develop a Super Power Memory and Get On in the World". Hard work, I can tell you, but I enjoyed every minute of it. Passed out after a while with 100 per cent.

What's that? You say you're interested? Great! Well, the name of the course escapes me just now, but I'll look it up for you, George.

Eh? Oh! Sorry, old chap! It's Charlie, of course! But watch that TV programme. I promise you'll learn a lot from it, like me. Well, must go. Lovely to see you again, Dave. Hope I've been of some help!

(Henry, back on the street:) Damn! Now where was I going before I bumped into old what's-his-name?

5

A Visit to Mumbles Pier

A mystery trip took me to Mumbles Pier, which I had often heard about and frequently seen from a distance. Older members of my family had waxed lyrical whenever the subject arose, so I was excited at being afforded the opportunity of a visit.

I alighted from the bus above the Pier Hotel and descended the steep concrete road to the pier's root, a road which would almost certainly be dangerous in the wet and virtually impassable in snow.

I recalled how my father had expressed his delight at purposely stopping his Morris Ten halfway up to change gear, causing my mother to pray loudly and with great fervour in Welsh: "Oh Arglwydd, bydda gyda ni yn nawr! Bydda gyda pob un o ni, os gwellwch Chi fod yn dda!" (Oh Lord, be with us now! Please look after us all, if you will be so good.)

On being heard by the good Lord, she clouted Dadda furiously on the back with her umbrella once the slope had been safely negotiated, calling him a silly old fool and threatening to get out and walk the eight miles home to Bon-y-maen.

At the bottom of the slope, I was confronted by a building which suggested it had seen better days and now served as an amusement arcade. I decided that it was probably a replica of every other such establishment I had seen (though not frequented), and so passed it by.

I turned right and immediately took a healthy interest in a ladies loo—not that I'm in any sense peculiar, mind you, but it occurred to me that it was the first fortified "bog" I had ever seen outside of a castle. The men of Mumbles, I thought, must have been prepared to go to great lengths to defend their ladies' virtue, as the top of this edifice was embellished with battlements.

I had a fleeting if warped vision of them squatting behind these pillars—bows, arrows, and spears at the ready—as a train chugged to a halt a short distance away, laden with dangerous foreigners from Swansea ready to go on a rampage. Without the stout door, a pretty young lass, as yet intact, sobbed as she sought desperately to gain entry to the safe confines of the building and join the other women of Mumbles Head. But she was rejected because her only offering, a slightly bent penny, was not acceptable to the key box ruthlessly denying her access.

I paid Mr Peter Price a trivial sum for a ticket that authorised me to venture along the pier itself. I safely traversed a huge plastic guardian gorilla and dragon, which caused me to wonder if they really wanted any visitors there at all.

Taking in the construction, I noted a vast area of elaborately decorated, cast iron side panels and railings and marvelled at the vastly superior durability of this material compared to steel. Elsewhere, though, there was evidence of insidious decay.

Some men were engaged—in between World Cup matches—in pitting their wits against the residents of the deep, and I paused, admiring their patience and optimism. "Any joy?" I enquired of a tall, sandy-haired fellow as he carefully placed yet another morsel of bait on his hook.

"Bloody hopeless!" was the reply. "I've come down for some bass for tea, and all I've managed to catch are three starfish!"

"Afraid to go 'ome, he is," observed his companion. "His old girl punches her weight, see! If he's lucky, he'll just catch the village fishmonger before he closes!"

I moved on and out along a lateral walkway to the famous lifeboat house. This at least appeared to have lost nothing over the years. As I stood at the door, regretting that it was locked, I became aware of an aura surrounding the place, an aura of elation and emotion that seemed to encompass me too.

There was elation born of numerous victories for the crews who had ventured forth from this slipway in the most appalling weather conditions to snatch wretched seafarers from the vile tempests for which the Bristol Channel was notorious.

There was emotion over failing to save others that these men of Mumbles had readily risked their lives for. And then too, there was the ultimate loss, not many years past, when the long vigil of those waiting at this very spot and further out at the head of the pier had terminated in the realisation that William Gammon and the brave hearts of

Nab Rock and Thistleboon would not be coming back from the floundering *Samtampa* that night—nor any other night.

Out in the distance, just where the Sker Rocks dipped razor-sharp into the sea, they had willingly made the ultimate sacrifice, not a hundred and fifty yards from the shore and the headland where so many Porthcawl people shone the headlights of their cars out to sea, praying furiously and fruitlessly, willing both crews to survive the maelstrom that was Rest Bay. I remembered going there a few days afterwards, being able to walk almost all the way to the vessel, and thinking that perhaps no lives might have been lost at all if only the *Samtampa*'s crew had remained aboard. Terror, however, knows no logic.

Before returning to the pier proper, the engineer in me led me to a close study of two galvanised tanks slung outboard of the walkway. Were they fresh-water tanks? Fuel tanks for the lifeboat perhaps? I looked at the riserless valves, trying to gauge whether they were open or closed. Then it dawned on me that the pipeline was too big for water. I tried to trace it back to its source but lost sight of it under the pier. I made a mental note to look for some spot where it could readily be connected to a road tank car near the hotel when I returned.

One thing the pier had always offered was a breathtaking view of the immediate area and further afield. Nothing had changed in this regard. The lighthouse to the right stood proud on its prominent rock, surrounded by what must once have been manned gun emplacements. Once, too, this practical edifice itself had been manned, though it was aloof now and lonely in its automation.

To the left was the great sweep of the bay, at first somewhat pebbly, and off which dozens of pleasure vessels had recently been moored. Above, across the promenade and the road, the yacht clubs were still there with their jealously guarded memberships, though their charges were gone, claimed by Swansea Marina, a safer but much less magical haven.

Between this location and the lovely yellow sands, stretching all of three miles to the docks of the adjoining city, had been the famous oyster beds, still there when I was a child.

"What happened, Mr Price, what happened?"

My dad had mentioned steamers.

"Hasn't been one off the pier here for fifteen years or more, man," was the keeper's reply.

"Always worked in this area, have you?" I asked.

"Yes, sir. Worked as a barman, I did, for twenty years, over in the hotel there. Then they shifted me from by there to by here. Same company it is now, see."

"What was it like when you were a young man, then?"

"Oh! There were shows the full length of the pier, man. Punch and Judy and that sort of thing. And plenty of stalls for eats. Kids flew their balloons and kites from the pier, all the poles flew flags, and at night, the place was blazing with coloured lights. There's a funny thing, isn't it? They don't fly flags much now. It's as if everyone's ashamed to, somehow. Other countries I've seen are more proud and seem to have them everywhere." He shook his head, bemused.

"That's the inshore lifeboat station over there." He pointed out a building on the shore some three hundred yards away. "A rubber boat it is, but very useful, mind. The

49

crews are interchangeable. It's probably saved as many from drowning as the big boy over here."

"There must have been very many more visitors when the trains and steamers were running," I ventured inanely.

"Gosh, yes, man! As you can see, we have two ticket offices, but that one over by there hasn't been used for years now. Deuce, I'll tell you, I've seen queues stretching back up the slope and dozens of yards past the arcade sometimes! Never be the same again though, I don't suppose, but we haven't given up altogether. See all that rot out the end there, did you? Well, we're hoping for a grant from the lottery to fix it."

I retraced my steps along the boards again. On one side of the structure, seagulls screeched and jostled querulously on railings, like schoolchildren trying to find a spot on the floor at assembly. Or maybe I was misinterpreting things, and they were actually voicing their objection to my venturing into what they probably considered their exclusive domain.

On the other side, on a girder way over the water, a lone gull, almost surely a lady bird, nestled on a few tufts of grass that was her home. She watched me but made no attempt to move as I approached within a few feet of her. She sensed somehow that I bore her and the still-encapsulated miracle beneath her no malice.

A young, attractive, and talented university tutor I knew strode purposefully back and forth. Was she merely savouring the pleasure of taking the fresh air that this aspect of her work afforded her? Or was she revelling in the agony she had inflicted on her brood of adults, most much older than herself, by landing them with the task of describing this place as a writing project?

What other agonies had these boards seen, I wondered? Had the pier provided balm to lonely hearts, earthing feelings of fear or hatred or rejection that had seeped through its turnstiles with souls in turmoil? Had it helped to blow away the confusion and clutter of mental cobwebs, providing a vital unblocking process essential for the success of optimistic students impatient to get on?

Out at sea, a coastal tanker headed for Swansea dock or Baglan Bay, and a pilot's cutter creamed through the water to meet it. Further out, almost enshrouded in maritime mist, a huge ore carrier—high out of the water now, having disgorged her Spanish cargo at Port Talbot—thrust her way down channel for yet another tussle with the Bay of Biscay.

Time was running out. I negotiated the turnstile again, thanking Mr Price for his informative chat as I went. My steps took me past the fortified loo, tranquil now the trains had been repulsed, my vision no longer warped. And so up the slope to the bus stop. At the top, I looked back and pondered.

Sure, I'd seen someplace new to me, and I was grateful for the opportunity. And sure, one couldn't have asked for a nicer day to visit. But Mumbles Pier, just the same, had been a disappointment. Times change, and its heyday was over. It was dying. It still undoubtedly administered balm to restless souls, and the odd bass or Swansea Bay whiting to more placid beings. Too, there was the unquestioned value of providing access to the sea for the lifeboat. But was that enough to persuade the hard-headed businessmen who allocated donations from the nation's punters that the pier was a cause worthy of their consideration?

If money of any consequence was forthcoming at all, I felt it would be much more charitable to use it for some amputation work. Dismantle the dereliction of the head, terminate the structure a little way past the lifeboat causeway, and save a huge sum of money. For the dodge 'em cars would no longer joust at its seaward end, nor steamers tie up again, irrespective of how much restorative work was done.

"What's the use, Mr Price? What's the use?"

6

Stand Back

Wife:	There you go again, changing the TV station without asking if I'm watching the programme on this one!
Husband:	But the football will be on in a minute!
Wife:	That's all you seem to think about—football, rugby, and the pub.
Husband:	OK then. You see what you want to see, and I'll go upstairs and watch the match up there.
Wife:	Yes, that's right! Clear off and leave me on my own again. I seem to spend half my life by myself!
Husband:	I'll tell you what. Let's record the football match, and I'll go and make you a cup of tea while you're watching your film. How does that grab you?
Wife:	You don't understand, do you? That's exactly the same as leaving me on my own. Gosh, you're stupid sometimes!

Husband: Bloody hell, woman! Can't I do anything to please you? What the devil's wrong with you? I'm trying to be reasonable, can't you see?

Wife: Go on. That's you all over! Lose your rag and start shouting! I expect you'll be hitting me next.

Husband: I'll do a damned sight better than that, sweetheart. Keep out of the way—TV tubes explode like a bomb when they get a boot through them!

7

It, Things, and Non-Things

I first heard about "things" when, as a very young lad about two years ago, I went with Mam in our trap one Sunday afternoon to tea at Aunt Myfannwy's in Llanbeddau.

I remember her saying to Mam, distinct, that some people of this "things" breed or sect had come to live in the town. We learned that they managed a couple of roundabouts in a fairground in Carmarthen and got their music either from honky-tonks or hurdy-gurdies—I forget which now.

Aunt Myfanwy went on to say that they had appeared nice and tidy when they first arrived, and the president of the Manuod Y Dref (definition further on) thought, on first scrutiny anyway, that they really might be quite the thing.

No one in Llanbeddau could make heads or tails of what they were talking, not even the few in the town who had learned to speak English. And, of course, nobody knew at the time what they did do for a livelihood either!

The Reverend Llewellyn Williams-Jones, MA, BD—him what said from his pulpit that he had become a man of the world quick after standing in for a fortnight as a preacher to sailors at London Docks—thought that they were actually "cockaninnies". Mother wondered what part of the globe they could have come from. Uncle Morgan said that they might be from the other side of the Severn, on the banks of another river called "Thames", where the capital was supposed to be.

Cousin Emrys, being well read, said he was sure that the name of the river was "Thomas", not "Thames", as everywhere was Welsh in the reign of Queen Boa-di-Seea, whose grandfather, as everybody knew, had been born in Ystrad Mynach.[3]

Aunt Myfanwy warned Uncle Morgan to be careful who was about when he mentioned capitals, even if he felt certain that he was right. She reminded him that his left eye had only just begun to heal after the last time he had told this opinion—in the Bryn Tegyll Arms on St David's Eve, of all times—and that was two months ago!

Cousin Emrys said that if Uncle Morgan had come home dead that night, Aunt Myfanwy would have skinned him alive. Fancy Uncle Morgan having the nerve to say his opinion in earshot of John-Willie, the Llanbeddau Cruiser Bruiser,[4] and his big brother Hopkin, him what had worn a size-eight shirt for Wales, according to Emrys, who knew

---

[3] Source: "Commy Coots for Little Crwts", Williams Press (LanfairPG) and Grandson, vol. 2785, page 182, col. 3 (halfway down).

[4] See *Who's Who and What's What in Llanbeddau*, up the back of the book.

damned well where the real capital was and make no mistake about it!

Cousin Emrys said Uncle Morgan had been very brave, both about what he had said and over his shiner. When John-Willie and Hopkin had gone on holiday to their gran in Llanelli, Uncle told Emrys that the Bruiser had hit him while he was blinking, which was definitely against the laws of the Kingsberry Rulers.

The following knowledge came from Cousin Emrys's standard-three notebook on the subject of historics, which encouraged research and asked scholars' opinions on why "things"—and non-things, I expect—developed as they did.

The Kingsberry Rulers
(Pugeelistic Lawmakers, etc.)

These people live in a big house called Buckingham Place up London, and everybody their way is envious of them as they are lucky enough to live at the bottom of the street from a posh famous lady what is known as "Pol the Mol". They must be quite the thing, as they go up Pol the Mol's place often. They always take their horses and carts with them, in case these get pinched while they are out. Some do say that the men what ride the horses are from out foreign, as they shout in a squeaky language to each other.

They are also a bit shady, and Mr George, the owner of the house and the horses and carts and things, has given them all fur caps to put on, for them not to be recognised easy. All these men are big and gigantic, and when not exercising the nags up and down the street in front of Pol the Mol's—where they make an awful, terrible mess—they are lounging around Mr George's place.

Mr George have put crates around his home for them to shelter in if it comes to rain, because his family won't have them in the house, not on any account. This is probably because they do stink something terrible of horses, and if they had to have the windows open all day, the rain would ruin their curtains and they would all catch bron-cossis in winter.

NB: None of the books in the school library tell where these curtains was bought, but Mrs Nellie Leyshon, chairperson of the Manuod Y Dref Subcommittee for Distribution of Ex-Second-Hand Clothes and Wellingtons to the Lanbeddau Nee-Dee and Knee Deep, said they couldn't have been much cop if they wouldn't stand up—or hang down—to a drop of water now and again.

Mrs Salli Rhys said she had heard that they were exactly all alike throughout Buckingham Place and had most likely come from a job lot bought in a lane up by there where they also sold petticoats. Mrs Rhys's younger brother Walli had told her that everything in this lane was cheap at half the price, and that was why you could get a lot with each lot for so little.

This BP family, and them of their ancestors what wasn't broke, actually used to manage armies, knights, peasants, and suchlike. Many of these suchlikes were shot to order or for not obeying orders and it now looks as if the family have been reduced to horse racing, carriage riding and managing boxers which they probably find easier to control than the other lot because they are willing to fight according to the Kingsberry Rulers.

There are still some pretty powerful folks in the house though, which they say has got more rooms than any of the happy-tats in Llanbeddau. This is probably because they have to put up the seconds and refs sometimes as well. It is unknown who made this room tally for sure, but it may be in a book called "Doomsday".

Old Mr Dodderidge, who is minding the Llanbeddau Public Library while Miss Peggy Richards, BA (Hons) Wales, is away getting more stock, said he had heard of the Doomsday Book but couldn't remember if he had read it at all. He looked all over the history and accountancy shelves but couldn't find it, and guessed that it must be out with someone. He put my name down on the wanted list so I would be first to have it when it came back. I was very proud to see it indeed, because I knew all the busybodies of Llanbeddau looked at the list regular, to find out what people were into, or about to get into, or trying to get out of. It said, "*Doomsday Book*—urgently required for historical research purposes by Master Emrys Prend-Y-Gast Jenkins, Esq."

Old Mr Dodderidge suggested to come back in a few days, when Miss Peggy Richards, BA (Hons) Wales, would be there, because she was miraculous with books and had even got one out of print called *Just-Asian Periods for Farmers*.

I asked old Mr Dodderidge, for my hysterical purposes, what did Just-Asians mean?

He asked me first what is my age and then told me in a bit of a whisper that they were those people what was of mixed blood, like Anglo-Indians, Hong Conguls, and Englishmen. Many of their ladies were very beautiful when their faces wasn't veiled. He said that he had seen some of them when he was in the army up the Oogli, and there were plenty in Mespot and London as well.

Way back in the good old days (near the end of the ancient ages era), a very handy person had took the trouble to write down in this Doomsday Book how many huts, rooms, windows, acres, rods, poles, and fish there was in the land, such as perch, salmon, and kippers. He was one of them authors what became famous after death, the same as happened to an abattoir owner called Francis Bacon. Some do say that the author of the Doomsday Book was actually a Froggy called William who was already famous as the conkers champion of France.

Mrs Sarah Annie Hicks said that she thought they had pretty peculiar ideas up London—things unheard of! She said no decent, God-fearing folks in Llanbeddau would ever dream of putting up such men as those shadies and refs and seconds in their homes. Imagine one running up and down her garden in football knickers, blowing his whistle to make sure the pea wasn't sticking, and stepping all over the tea roses and carrots. Her man Gomer would have forty fits in his grave, poor dab!

Granny Thomas said it wouldn't do Sarah Hicks much good either, not with her galloping heartbeat. Old Mam Bethan, in a rare moment of lucy-ditty, thought that they had lower standards up London because they weren't Welsh Methodists nor even Baptists or Congregats, and that the Manuod y Dref should pray solemn for them to save their souls.

The ladies of the Manuod y Dref (definition not far off now) had become quite educated after agreeing to take a closer interest in their children's schoolwork. Also, they had become very mancy-pated, supporting Lizzie Lil Lloyd, her who was called Lazy Lil at one time for not keeping her front doorstep scrubbed. This was because she had got polly ticks in her system, which made some of the lower-educated ladies scratch like the dickens at the mention of her.

Then they heard that Lizzie Lil had been shouting up London for all their rights in Welsh, and had got herself chained to the fences at Buckingham Place and Parley-Ment as well as getting her jib in some of the papers up there. They rallied round her straight away, of course—but not too close, as Horace Jones the vet explained that ticks could jump like scalded cats on you easy.

The Manuod y Dref (explanation shortly) decided to pass a resolution to stamp their feet down heavy on all things unheard of, after listening to a lecture on "The Control of Male Hormone Sapiens and Other Vermin" by Dame Emily Tucker, a big lady from Cardiff pro-cured by Lizzie Lil.

Applying the principles suggested by Dame Emily, they said that the only decent places for such as visiting refs etc. were the football gear shed on the edge of Llanbeddau Rugby/Football Pitch or Fat Mary Lou's Fourpenny Doss House at Number Two Railway Arches. (Sheets changed regular on the first Monday of every month.) See *Who's Who and What's What and Why in Wales*, up the back pages. Researched by Standard Three, Llanbeddau Primary School Teacher, Elyder Bowen EdCert.

Apparently, this Mr George of Buckingham Place don't call hisself "Mister"! He actually do sign all his papers and letters "George V". The school do all think this is an affliction because everybody up by his place know that his real name is Mr Rex George. Standard three think he is probably relatived to Lloyd George, The Earl of Dwyfor. The Earl of Dwyfor knows my dad and my dad do know the earl. He has seen him canvassing for the Liberals plenty of times round our way, so he said.

NB: These canvasses by the earl are very rare and they never see the light of day. Class thinks they must be special like them of Michael Angeloff's if the Liberals pretend they never heard of them, but I don't know how they can say such blateful lies when others have seen him at it. I heard Dad telling our mam that he was "at it" pretty often.

Historicle Observation: Some book said that artists should not hide their candles under bushes. One hundred per cent of class think this is right because of the risk of fire if somebody cranky lit them.

Mr Rex is descended from the Planta-Jeanettes, and some do say these Jeanettes (or Jeans) got in his blood from the Tudors, which is probable why he do call his hair the Prince of Wales.

Everyone in Buckingham Place is royalist down to their bootstraps. Mr George have given many of them and their pals chitties called war-rants.

I could see that Cousin Emrys was a good historical researcher for his class, as Mr Elyder Bowen EdCert had written at the bottom of this exercise book in red ink:

"Fascinating revamp of important periods in British history. Near the mark in places (give or take a century). Can barely wait to read your interpretation of this week's study lesson on the Battle of Agincourt and compare your work with William Shakespeare's."

I asked Cousin Emrys who was this Shakespeare and he said that he thought that he was one of them snobby prefects in standard six, where there was supposed to be one or two pupils who were also sharp on histrionics like all the scholars in standard three.

The subject of Uncles Morgan's fight came up again when he, Cousin Emrys, and I went out the garden to see Uncle's pigeons after tea. I learned that Mr Tim Tammer,[5] the Llanbeddau blacksmith and a local referee of note, had had to officiate and hold Uncle back hard. I heard that he had only just managed to stop Uncle Morgan from half killing John-Willie and Hopkin together.

Uncle Morgan made Cousin Emrys and me promise faithful on our honour and hope to die that we would not breathe a word of this anywhere near John-Willie or Hopkin, as half killing, like proper killing, was against the rules. The boxer and his brother might get upset and want to take Uncle up in front of a beak.

Uncle Morgan pointed out that bygones should be bygones and water under a bridge somewhere or other, but I forget now if he said where it was.

Excitedly, I told Mam all about the fight when we went in. Aunt Myfanwy made a face and said she didn't think John-Willie nor his brother would bother about no beak,

---

5 See *Who's Who* etc. up the rear.

least aways not before they had attended to Uncle's other eye first!

———————————◂ ◂ ▸ ▸————————————

It didn't dawn on the Hi-raquey and inhabitants of Llanbeddau that the capital cockaninnies weren't the real thing until these non-things tried to repair a broken honky-tonk, or perhaps it was one of their hurdy-gurdies, in a field behind Lady Priscilla Gwendraeth Hughes's home one Sunday morning. Having fixed it one way or another (Cousin Emrys said it was squealing blue murder like a porker being terminated by Davies the butcher), they had the insensey-tivity to take it away in a gaudy, bawdy truck with scantily clad, though bountifully equipped dancing girls painted on the sides—just as everyone was coming out of chapel!

It was a big meeting Sunday too. The ladies were wearing their best and biggest hats, and their husbands had taken time to polish the chains of their Alberts. The ladies had all been disgusted at the sight. "Just imagine, my dear, what a terrible shock it must have been for the weaker and meeker ones!" said Aunt Myfanwy (referring to the menfolk and children).

Mam was nearly wetting herself with the excitement of it all. "Go on! Go on, Myfanwy!" she squeaked, forgetting that Emrys and I were there.

"Well, it wasn't only that," continued Aunty. "But you know, the ladies had to take their hats off to shield the delicate eyes of their children from the paintings. Some of them had their hair fall down, poor dabs, as their hat pins were also holding up their buns! The preacher and the deacons didn't know where to look, because the driver stopped to let the congregation cross the road, and it took three times longer than normal for peeping, d'you see! The men were twice as worse than the children, girl. Terrible, it was. Yes indeed!"

Mam agreed. "Yes, yes undeed! Er, what happened then, Myfanwy?"

Aunt Myfanwy went on with her story, and I listened maximum volume. Apparently, the first to recover was the chief of the elders, Mr Randolph Edwards, known behind his back in Aunty's chapel as "Handy Randy" because of being good at doing things or getting things done—like having slates replaced on the vestry roof, comforting village widows, and organising Band of Hope picnics to Tenby every year.

Aunt Myfanwy was famous for challenging Mr Edwards in chapel one Sunday after he had made the announcement about the annual trip, just before taking the collection. She stood up and told him that it was the belief of the mothers' circle of the Manuod y Dref that he was either totally devoid of imagination, or Tenby was an angler's paradise!

In this august sororihood, the mothers' circle was one level below the grandmothers' circle—though a lot more productive, of course, 'specially in thinking up things to make and do. (Some more info on the Manuod y Dref further on.)

"Go on, Myfanwy," urged Mam impatiently. "What else happened outside the chapel then? What did Handy Randy do, girl?" But Aunt Myfanwy was well into her argument about the Band of Hope and was determined to finish.

The mothers' circle thought that there was something pretty fishy about half the men in Llanbeddau belonging to the Band of Hope, especially as several boozers who never went near chapel otherwise always paid their subs on the dot, and were usually first on the charabanc as well.

"My dear," Aunty went on, "these men had so much tackle with them last year that some of the older teen boys had to stand up all the journey. They were so fagged out when they got to Tenby that they couldn't enjoy themselves on the beach with the rest of the chapel folk. They said they just wanted go and lay down among the sand dunes to get over it!"

Anyway, she said that she was encouraged by all the women in chapel nodding their heads delicately over what she had told Mr Randolph Edwards, though really, they wanted to nod like mad.

It should be noted that nodding like mad, cheering, and clapping (slow or furious) was forbidden in Welsh chapels after the introduction of the electric light, so as not to break the glass. Choirs had to have as many altos and baritones as they had tenors and sopranos for the same reason. The originator of the idea had been the chief army chaplain in Pont-y-Cherri out India way. He mentioned it at a Methodist rally after a light bulb nearly fell on his head as the choir hit top note together, singing "When up high we all doth go."

"It's a bit like soldiers having to change step when crossing a bridge," he pointed out. "To stop it falling down to the depths where Satan is waiting, you see!"

Uncle Morgan said they hadn't had any trouble like this when they had paraffin lamps, but Aunt Myfanwy felt electrics was better all round as they didn't have so many bad "coffins" in chapel and the kiddies made less noise through not needing so many sweets.

———————◆ ◆ ◆ ◆———————

Mam steered her sister back to the goings on outside the chapel. "Well," Aunty said, "Mr Randolph Edwards rushed over to the cockaninny lorry and, flinging his overcoat wide open, tried to cover one of the nubile maidens, to cheers from some of the older youngsters."

"Never!" said our mam, shocked. "There's naughty of them, isn't it! What happened then, Myfanwy?"

"Well, I was with Lady Priscilla Gwendraeth Hughes by the chapel gates, and she said it was the sort of manly action to be expected of Mr Randolph Edwards. But if they hadn't known who he was, what he did could easily have been misunderstood."

Aunt Myfanwy had agreed with this scenty-ment, 'specially as he had been facing the lorry and had called another elder to come and give him a lift up because the maidens were high off the ground. She said the two elders were there for ages, stopping the driver from returning the hurdy-gurdy to the cockaninnies in Carmarthen until everyone was safely out of sight.

Mrs Leticia Edwards, the chief elder's wife, had later reported to the Manuod Disciplinary Panel that she had burned the overcoat to cinders as she thought that it had been defiled. It was only six years old, too, having been bequeathed to Mr Randolph Edwards by his uncle Dai,[6]

---

[6] See *Who's Who*, up the end.

the well-known secretary of the Llanbeddau Whippet and Pigeon clubs.

The birds, or perhaps it was the dogs, or even both, had been instree-mental in Dai suffering from two fatal deceases that could kill you, according to Emrys, who told me their medicinal names. He had a "doolalee tap" which was faulty, giving him lots of problems with water trouble. And he had a nasty "silly coo-cyst" on his chest that he probably got cleaning out the pigeon loft. Dai, I was told, had patiently and courageously borne them on his broad shoulders for ages. While performing this feat, he had managed to kick a bucket to somewhere and could boast when he died that he had the biggest funeral ever seen in the district.

Uncle Morgan had told Cousin Emrys that the corset had stretched back round all the seven bends in the road to the cemetery. Cousin Emrys also said Dai had gone west like a light and had died with his best shoes on.

Uncle Morgan told Mam that there was no doubt at all about Dai Edwards holding the record, as the number of bends that a man's funeral cortege took up down Cemetery Road was incised in ogi-marks on the headstone of his grave, right where it do say RIP in Welsh. The hearse horse was always stopped at the graveyard entrance for the undertaker's assistant to pedal back on his bike and make a check for Daniel Dickins, the stonemason.

Dai had even beaten Lady Priscilla's grandfather, Sir Paul, who had been a Whig or a bigwig or had worn a wig or something up the capital. It seems that when the Sir decided to go out west—Cousin Emrys thought he might have been one of those pioneers like Wyatt Earp, Buffalo Bill, and some famous people as well—two trainloads of supporters arrived from London to see him off, scoring him six and a half bends in Cemetery Road and sixty-five ogi-marks on his gravestone—a figure unbeaten before!

Eight Sir Paul-bearers came from two of the pubs up there called Grey's Inn and Lincoln's Inn, and Uncle had been dying to ask if any of them had a handy skittles team. Then he thought in view of the sir-come-tances, he better hadn't.

Confidentally, Aunt Myfanwy told Mam that the elders of her chapel had been at their wits' ends for months in case someone even more popular or important died, as there wasn't any more bends in the road to the graveyard. However, she herself didn't see that there was anything to get excited about, as there was nobody in the Offing[7] so far as she knew, and as deputy of the Manuod, there wasn't much she didn't know about important things like that.

Uncle Morgan chuckled, adding that the problem had been solved in the Bryntegyll Arms one night by Douglas "The Digit" Watkins, maths teacher of Ysgol Y Bechgyn Llanbeddau (Llanbeddau Boy's School). "Doug the Dig," as he was known to everyone, said there was nothing to lose any sleep over. The answer was staring them all in the face. All they had to do when the time came was take in a circuit of the duckpond near the cemetery entrance as well, if the assistant signalled that the tail of the funeral was stretching back to where the eighth bend would have been if there was one. Eight bends would be equal to a circle mark on the stone.

---

[7] I must remember to ask Cousin Emrys what and where this Offing place is.

This was overheard by one of the chapel elders, who just happened to call in for medicinal purposes and who took some of the credit for recognising logic in the suggestion. Fair play to him, though, he had also given a bit of credit to Mr "Digit" Watkins as well.

According to Uncle, the set fawr of elders (similar to a pride of lions, but in chapel) had been so relieved that that they had totally forgot to question their peer on the precise medicinal benefits of double gins. They had, in fact, offered to put Doug the Dig on the shortlist of replacement elders. Emrys told me that this shortlist was a very important document which was kept safe in a safe and only saw the light of day when an elder's lights went out. It was pointed out that Doug would have to join the Band of Hope, of course, but as an elder, he would be entitled to such perks as free trips.

However, in their eagerness to show gratitude, the Methodist elders had forgot the very important fact that Doug was a Baptist. Although it was jolly nice of them, he said, there was no way he was going to change his religion, not for all the tea in China nor umpteen pieces of silver shekels—both of which sounded a heck of a lot to me!

The Methodist elders were very saddened, as they only wanted to show their appreeshi-ayshon by giving him their highest local award—well, next to actually making him an elder, that is, isn't it?

On telling about the offer to his own pastor, Doug was delighted to hear there was nothing stopping him having honorary Methodist elder status, so long as he didn't spend no more time in their chapel than he did in his own, like. Indeed, his pastor also said that when he was younger and serving chaplain up Bengal, he had got hisself four or five honorary elderships of different kinds. He had akchewally fouled the head chaplain once, who had casty-gated him when, in his efforts not to seem toffee-nosed, he had almost took up eldership with some non-believing believers as well!

I can still see Mam wriggling with excitement in Aunt Myfanwy's Chipperfield chair as she listened to all the drama. "Good gosh! Nothing like this ever happens in our place. No indeed, girl, never! It's all go in Llanbeddau, isn't it? Our place do seem like the graveyard in comparison. I can't wait to tell my Dick [my dad]. We do never have such fun as this!"

More tea was poured all round in Aunt Myfanwy's shell-e cups. Aunt Myfanwy was very posh. Mam said she had a matched tea set, and she and Uncle Morgan had a lav with fancy paper in the house. Though my dad said this was unhigh-jeannick and should be at the bottom of the garden like ours, with quartered pieces of the *Echo* on a nail.

Our mam had another go at getting Aunt Myfanwy going on what happened after the big meeting. It seems when the Manuod Disciplinary Panel heard of the destruction of Mr Randolph Edwards' raglan overcoat, they had given Mrs Randolph Edwards six approbationary claps for determination. Indeed, Lady Priscilla and Aunt Myfanwy had agreed that Mrs Randolph Edwards could have qualified for a dozen claps if she hadn't allowed Handy Randy to wear it until the cold snap was over.

Uncle Morgan said he wasn't sure whether the truck driver had been advertising or was natural polite, but Aunt Myfanwy was certain sure in her own mind that he had stopped to advertise the scanties, and politeness had nothing to do with it She wasn't daft nor born last month, she said, even if Uncle Morgan did think so.

Cousin Emrys told me afterwards that she had given Uncle hell when they got home because he and some other men had gone back and fore across the road several times to hurry the children to safety while watching the lorry carefully, in case it shifted.

Mam was told that the ladies had got a hastily arranged men's darts match between Llanbeddau and a pub in Carmarthen "cancelled until further notice". Aunt Myfanwy, speaking as deputy president to Lady Priscilla at the Manuod Y Dref (explain-nation now really immy-nent), said that this could be took by the dartsmen as "binding solid" so long as the cockaninnies and their roundabouts, hurdy-gurdies, and scanties remained in Carmarthen.

8

The Manuod y Dref

The Manuod y Dref, Uncle Morgan explained to Emrys and me, was a mighty strong female body with powers that terrified most of the men around the country. But we were a bit too young for him to tell us why this was, exactly. The way he told us, I didn't know what to imagine, but Emrys whispered to me that they had a lot of muscle and he had heard them called "The Terrible Taffeta Tafia".

Menfolk were very wary what they said because the Manuod had been fillyated at some time or other to another strong body up England way (sex unknown). When Aunt Myfanwy wasn't listening, Uncle Morgan told us that the Manuod were very secretive and not many men knew what went on behind the closed doors of the Llanbeddau Institute when they were in session. All they could be sure of was that it was a place where a lot of orders came from, and it seemed very often indeed that the Manuod were more powerful than the town council itself. If the mayor was told by the Manuod to jump, he usually jumped pretty damned high, and all the members of the council jumped with him!

Emrys whispered that his sister Rhiannon was in the girls' section and was due to go to an annual camp in Llangronack, where she would undergo initiation in a tent so that she could be elevated to the women's section when she was eighteen. When she eventually got married and had babies, she would join the mothers' section.

There was also a ladies' section. You had to be on a commit- tee to be a lady, but once you were ladyfied, you stayed one for life and thereafter. If you got chucked off a committee, you became a "past lady".

(Here endeth the promised explanation and description of the Manuod y Dref.)

Gobaeth Smith, a twice-removed cousin of Uncle Morgan's and a miners leader from the valleys, said the men up there were made of sterner stuff and had got on top of their Manuod fairly quickly when they started kicking up trouble. But he admitted that their ladies hadn't given in without a terrific struggle, according to what Cousin Emry heard him tell Uncle Morgan.

The valley men had had to have a number of meetings underground in order to plan a strata-tidgey and be sure that any ideas and suggestions did not leak back to the Manuod, as had happened when the meetings were held at the pitheads. The comrades had discovered at that time that there were Manuod spies around in the form of their very own daughters, who had been told to be "all ears" when they took butties and beer to their dads and brothers at mid-shift.

Gobaeth Smith was willing, while visiting Llanbeddau, to give the miners' lodge there the benefit of his experience, but Uncle Morgan had been dubey-assed about it. He felt sure that the Llanbeddau men would want to fight their own fight and were quite capable of manhandling their Manuod y Dref without help from other comrades.

———◆ ◆ ◆———

While Uncle Morgan took Cousin Emrys to trumpet practice in the Morris Eight, Mam asked Aunt Myfanwy how the men had reacted to the Manuod putting the kai-bosh on their gally-vantincks and folldee-rols. We heard that Uncle Morgan had been approached, as the husband of the deputy president of the Manuod, to explain on the men's behalf that there had been no ulteria motifs. Indeed, he was to point out that the ladies should have known their loved ones more better than to support a motion by Mrs Gwilliam "Ty Bachty" Farm that they were all a pack of old schemers and not to be trusted one jot or tittle!

Uncle was to tell her about the men's bitter disappointment at over this lack of trust. Indeed, their chairman, Mr Brindley Morris Jones, had personally come up to Aunt Myfanwy's house, looking like thunder. With the parlour door shut, he had briefed Uncle Morgan on what had to be said on behalf of the pub committee.

Aunt Myfanwy had crept into the passage and listened on her knees to what was going on through the keyhole. She told Mam it had cost her a pair of best stockings new from Ben Evans' store in Swansea, but indeed to goodness, it had been worth every damaged dernier, she said.

"We aren't all randy farmers like Gwilliam Ty Bachty," shouted Brindley Morris Jones. "Everyone knows he's a bit of a stinker. Any man who makes his own beer and can't throw a double top with thirty-three darts, leave alone three, is understandably a candidate for Mrs Gwilliam's motion and a hundred per cent show of hands or legs or whatever they show in the Manuod y Dref to display their feelings."

"Here, here, indeed, man," Uncle said. "But keep your voice down in respect for my house, boy. On your side I am, isn't it? You're in the home of the vice president of the Manuod, don't forget. Walls do have ears round by here for goodness sake!"

"Brindley calmed down a bit then and apologised," recounted Aunt Myfanwy, "but he was pretty upset and his voice was still halfway up the wall, girl. I was expecting my Morgan to plonk him for yelling in our parlour, and portraits of Morgan's mother and father hanging up in there listening too!"

As Aunty told it, Brindley Morris Jones went on, "Well, I knew you were one of us, Morgan bach, and we all understand your position here—in the lioness's den, so to speak. You are a brave man indeed. But to think that the Manuod could do such a thing as not trusting their menfolk and cancelling our trip, man! Us who they had chosen to father their offspring too. Well, on behalf of the club and the pub, I have to say I am totally appalled, both completely and utterly!"

Mam put her hand to her mouth in shock. "Never, our Myfanwy! He didn't really say that, did he?"

"Oh yes he did! And something else too. A completely and utterly appalled Brindley Morris Jones is a terrible sight to behold, I can tell you!" She nodded her head vigorously, certain sure, having seen him herself.

But the Manuod y Dref would not be shifted from the position they had adopted, and in the end, in deffyrence to their wishes, the men had voted to use the money they had collected on a men's only mystery trip in Shadrac Owen's charabang instead.

Mrs Shadrac Owen had been called in straight away by the Manuod Panel for the Regulation and Control of Llanbeddau Males to show them a charabang schedule. "And do you know what?" said Aunt Myfanwy. "It didn't mention no mystery trip" for that day at all, girl! It just showed a regular run to Manorbier. Shadrac had told his wife to say that the regular trip had got to be cancelled, unfortunately, because it was a bank holiday. The market would be closed, so the trip would be uneconomical."

Uncle was asked to talk to Aunt Myfanwy, in her important capacity, to sound out a new idea which had been put forward. There would be quite a bit of the collected money left over from this new trip, as it was cheaper. So the men had agreed to a lovely suggestion by Charlie Thomas, the treasurer (whom they all knew was afraid of his missus), that they buy little momen-to gifts for the ladies, wherever it was the mystery would land up. Please could Aunt Myfanwy approach the ladies on this point pretty quick, because it was rumouring that a glee party and its supporters from Haverfordwest were also after the charabang.

Shadrac Owen had said he would prefer to go with the Llanbeddau Darts team, all of who were his butties, although he was also partial to a bit of glee, too, mind, but at the right time and place, isn't it?

Uncle was to take special care to mention to Aunty that the Reverend Llewellyn Williams-Jones, MA, BD, was also going on the mystery trip, along with five of the chapel elders. As soon as they heard this, the Manuod called an emergency meeting to say, "The men can all go, bless them, and how thoughtful about the expensive presents they will be bringing back for their wives and all their lovely children!"

On the morning of the mystery trip, Shadrac had some very sad news to tell the men. The charabang was oversupscribed as it had just come under a new government law saying that it was no longer allowed to have anybody standing in a charabang or omnibus with solid tyres. Constable Corbin of the county constabby-larry (Corb the Stab) was going too, and Shadrac could not risk his bread and butter.

Sorry, indeed! But in order to keep his licence clean and let him safely service the community so close to his heart, he had got to call for six volunteers with the generosity of spirit to stay behind The six who did were sure to have free rides and return to anywhere on the next day's schedule, compliments of the pub committee.

This plea was, of course, way up in chapel territory, and the noble preacher and his elders responded immediately, as if it were a Band of Hope clarion call, according to Uncle Morgan.

"Bless them also," said Brindley as the old bus wheezed its way up the hill out of Llanbeddau. "Next stop, Carmarthen Fair!"

Well, even without severe rebukes and thunder and lightning from the pulpit, it was inevitable that the Manuod would come to hear of it sooner or later. It wasn't too long before Mrs Shadrac Owen, a director of the charabang company, was back on the carpet. She explained, "Well, it was like this, Madam President. The day before the mystery trip was my Shadrac's day off for vehicle maintenance, and he had to re-adjust his carburettor and fix some trouble with the autovac.

"Shad planned to take the men to Cardigan, but when they had only gone halfway, the autovac started to give trouble again with the splutters. Like the good old rugby player that he is, love him, my dear, considerate Shad decided to play for touch, isn't it? He headed for Carmarthen instead, where the men thought he was much more sure to find the spares they were looking for, you see!"

The Manuod y Dref accepted the explanation, though Aunt Myfanwy told Mam that Madam Secretary had written "with gravest doubts" after this point in the minute book, because several members weren't very happy about where Shadrac had had to go to put the charabang right.

"Did they know," asked one member who was born in Carmarthen, "that the garage was right behind the fairground?"

The ladies also expressed the hope that the "auto thingee bit" was now working proper, as none of them fancied walking home from Manorbier Market, rain or shine, just because a silly old piece like that was spluttering away like mad. As Megan Lewis, Penfilia House, pointed out, "Some of our ladies might be heavily laden."

Old Granny Watkins added, "Yes, indeed, and in more ways than one, thanks to those old devils, isn't it?"

In order to hear all the goings on in Llanbeddau, Mam and I had to stay on to supper, and it was nearly midnight when our trap, our horse Polly, and us got home. I could hear

Mam telling Dada all the Llanbeddau clecks for ages after they had put the candle out. I was so filled with admiration for Cousin Emrys and his knowledge, and Uncle Morgan and his guts, that I only managed to go to sleep as I was waking up. Well, so it did look like, anyway!

Mam said at breakfast next morning that she could hardly wait to pay Aunt Myfanwy and Uncle Morgan another visit. But she thought that it was best not for me to accompany her next time, as she felt very strongly that when disgusting things like "things" and things were being dis-gust, it wasn't quite the thing for young things like me to hear about them.

Cycle-lojically, I think this decision was bad for me, as I was very apree-hensitive of "it" and all manner of "things" afterwards—even "things unheard of" would scare me stiff!

End of Essay

———◆·◆·◆———

Class Teacher's Remarks

A very impressive work indeed, Brynmor. I am very proud of you. Providing your parents don't thrash you to death for writing about the family, and the Manuod y Dref don't demand your tummy for garters, you could well go to Oxford, even if only via Cardiff, Newport, and Gloucester by train. Keep it up!

PS: You may keep the inkwell.

———◆·◆·◆———

Llanbeddau Primary School
Standard Three Class History Research Dossier

Who's Who, What's What, and Why in Wales

Compiler in Chief: Master Emrys Prend y Gast Jenkins
(top of the class two years running)

Tucker, Emily Hortense, Dame

The Honourable Dame, 1921. Only daughter of Sir Biban Tucker, Baronet, and Lady Tucker of Twll Glo, Rhondda.

Made her name standing up for women up London. Became dishonourable for a time and was in a chain gang with Lizzie Lil Lloyd of Llanbeddau.

> Attitude to men: "I often have them for lunch, my dears. I must confess, I really do enjoy my males."
>
> Men's attitude to her: They make themselves scarce when she is about. They also pay her butlah backhanders for information from her appointments diary so they can steer clear. Source: third gardener's helper.
>
> Schooling: Cowbridge (starting), Cheltenham (finishing), Cambridge (ruining).
>
> Disposition: Fierce when sober (up to mid a.m.). Savaging men by lunchtime. She have canny-balistic ten dancys and have scored many hits on cabinet ministers with ripe tomatoes and rotten eggs. (NB: None of these ministers were Methodists.)

Dai-Mentions
> Up: 5 ft 1 in.
> Down: Ditto
> Across: 44 in. (lungs deflated)
> Over: Not known
> Riding boots: Size 11c
> Hat size: Private

> Riding Crop: Lead loaded. Supplied by David Evans, Leather Merchant, Newport, England.
> Interests (finanshal): From the Cymru Bank (Welsh Branch), Ely Avenue, Cardiff, Glamshire, and Shangri-La Bank, Marine Drive, Bomb Bay. Dines out at La Pozers, Tiger Bay. Breaks chains, bonds, and "things" and said to be gusty. Lectures all around, free of charge.
> Other: Got beat up by peelers but took out six, which class think is forgiving. Sent to House of Lords, Ladies, and Dames, out of harm's way, on request of her dad, who also knew Lloyd George.

Lloyd, Elizabeth Lilly, Mrs

A mancy-pated woman of Llanbeddau. Second child of Henri Leyshon, conductor (bus and choir), and Mrs Letti Leyshon, No. 2 Railway Cottages.

Dai-Mentions
> Weight (starkers): 8 st 2 lbs
> Height (in best hat): 6 ft (6 ft 6)
> Before meals: 33 in.–32 in.–33 in.
> Attitude to men: Fancies them

Attitude of Men: Nothing doing

Born honourably in the back room of her home and delivered by Mrs Llew Probert, SRN (midwife). Parents married ninety-two months earlier at Bethel, Capel y Methodistiad, Llanbeddau.

Later became dishonourable when she kicked over some ropes or something and ran away to join the Sufferin' Jet Movement up London to fight for freedom for the stronger sex. Got chained to the fence round Buckingham Place with Mrs Melee Pancake and Dame Emily Hortense Tucker of Porth. Also got assaulted by bobbies and peelers.

When she got back to Llanbeddau from the Sufferin' Jet Wars, she found that she was note horeous and quite famous too. Every mobile member of the Manuod y Dref was on the station to welcome her home with the Band of Hope flutes and tambourines and the Bryntegyll Arms Silver Band. They also got Dr Meredith standing by in a waiting room to give her a free checkout for fleas.

> Interesting Features: Visible chain burn marks on wrists, neck, and ankles. Tattoo signs of a senior sufferin' jet around vaccination marks.
>
> Honours: Gold medal with crossed truncheons of a high-pressure sufferin' jet; member of Llanbeddau Manuod y Dref for life and thereafter.
>
> Other: Packs tremendous punch as wife of mayor of Llanbeddau. She is also a mayoress.

Edwards, Dai, MM

Uncle to Randolph Edwards, eldest elder at Bethel Galvanised Methodist Chapel, Llanbeddau.

Civvy Street: Miner injured, 1919 pension.

Army Street: Sergeant major, wounded in 1914–18 war at Passion Dale Pension. One pukka military medal. Six union medals. Granted Freedom of Llanbeddau, 1920.

Other: Past president of the West Wales Miners Low-Level Society. Whippet owner and pigeon fancier. Was president of both clubs and a famous judge in the Welsh divisions. Wore bowler, waistcoat, spats, and albert when sitting in judgement. Suffered severe water trouble (leaking doolalee tap) and had a silly coo-cyst on chest. Funeral record holder of Llanbeddau and district (seven ogi-marks on headstone).

Dai-Mentions

Height: 5 ft 10 in.

Chest: 44 in. (without medals)

Inside leg:

Left: 23 in.

Right: 22 in.

(Due to pit and war injuries)

Deceased and diseased, and very popular alive and dead.

George Rex, Esq.

A top leader from the bottom of Pol the Mol's street address: 1 Buckingham Place, London.

Decorations: Everything made by Toye, Kensitas, and Spendthrift Ltd, such as KG, KT, KCMG, KSI, KIE, KKK, etc.

Tie-Tels: King, Emperor, Gaffer, Duc, Duke, Duque, Marquis, Marquee, Gov. Not a Sir yet, though most of his staff do call him that. School think that this is bad, as it could make him a bighead.

Background: Naval School. Think that he must be pretty old as there are lots of rings on his sleeves.

Married girl called Mary whose father was a teck (not known if Scotland Yard or a private eye). Mary must be pretty good about the house as her loving husband, Mr George, have made her responsible for carrying all the family issues, and they and all their issues have lived happily ever after. (Well, up till now, anyhow.)

Dai-Mentions

Robust. Quite tall in boots.

Features: Centre parting and pointed beard. Copies Kitchener and leans to port due to weight of sword. Often wears spurs but never in bed like his cousin, Kaiser Bill.

His pit, which he do share with Mary, is a four-masted doubler fitted with side curtains and mozzi netting.

Qualyfikesons: Archbishop's boss. Air, land, and naval marshal. Commonwealthy and uncommon wealthy. Also terrible shocking rich.

Properties: Dutch cheese of Cornwell and Llancaster, Delhi, Rangoon, Ali-Springs, Nye Robby, Vank Hoover, and Wigan Heights. Also has many sub Dutch cheeses in between and round the edges. All this do show his foreigner linny-age and some of his family background as well.

Mr George is not as wealthy as Former Lee, who had forty-five reggie-ments of foot, six reggie-ments of horse, ten squadrons of pups and camels, and small, medium, and big guns, such as colonels, generals, and railway-mounted 45s.

Mr George has a good few field marshals and lots of road marshals as well, who have to check the route before him and Mary go out in their carts. Some of these carts is made of gold, and he and Mary do own some of the best carthorses up London. Class heard it do take six hefty nags to pull them, as gold is so heavy.

Mrs Pol The Mol have gone one better, so they say, and have got a Daimler Benz Laudolette which takes twenty-five horses and a choffer to shift it when equipped with carbide lamps and self-starter. Going full pelt, this limo can do the full length of Pol the Mol's street in 120 seconds flat using its Bap-Bap Honking Apparatus to clear the way through the crowds.

Peckulyarities: There are some queer peckulyarities going on in Buckingham Place. People have heard that Mr G do wear a garter on one of his legs sometimes and collects metal hats. He can't keep these on long as: (1) they are pretty heavy, and (2) they might get nicked when he takes them off for a bit of a rest, as he keeps his gems in them for some reason—not in a box under the bed like us sensible folk down by here.

Mr George had three fethers and four fathers and they all wore the same sort of hats. Mr George do send out lots of orders. One of them is the Order of the Bath, for when he wants to get swilled down and made tidy before going out in his ermine coat. Class heard that this could do with a good wash too, as there are big spots on the collar in all the pictures took of him.

The baths up his place is all made of enamel, not tin like ours. Class think that enamel has disadvancings, the most impotent of which is that you can see the tide marks. Teacher said in the geografy lesson that they do have a lot of scum up London, and our preacher said he saw so much up there when he was working on the docks, that it was sinful.

Buckingham Place is loaded with gongs, tie-tels, and other trinkets which Mr George Rex gives away to his family and friends, and even other people when he do feel like it. Most folks are reluctant to take them, as he likes to play a joke on them before parting with the stuff. He do make them stoop on one knee and pretends to chop off their nuts with a sword to put the wind up them.

Granny Thomas said, "It do take all sorts!"

Richards, Pegwen (Peggy), BA (Hons)

Spinster, but not by design. Too clever. Llanbeddau born and bred.

Age: Mature

Appearance: Attractive. Gets lots of wolf calls regular. Source: our maths teacher.

Education: Llanbeddau Infants and Primary Schools, Fforrest High School for Girls, University of Wales–Aberystwyth.

Qalyfikesons: Well-equipped to get a man. (Source: Old Granny Thomas.) Spinster of Arts–Literature. Certified Licensiate of Literate Librarians (C treble L).

Skills: Miraculous with books and gets them out of stock and print. Makes good buttered Welsh cakes.

Attitude to men: Planned coy-ness

Attitude of men: Planned coit-ness also

Atri-butes: Secretary of the Llanbeddau Manuod y Dref, who are all looking around for her! (Source: Myfanwy Prend y Gast Jenkins, Esq-ess and vice president.)

Tammer, Timothy Egbert

Known as Tammer the Hammer, blacksmith of Llanbeddau. Son of Sam "The Wham" Tammer, RIP, and Mrs Florrie Tammer, RIP ditto.

Interests: Unofficial football official (reffi-ree—Sundays and bank holidays excepted). Owns sixteen pages of *Associated Football League Reffi-ree's Guide*, which blew off the top of a tramcar. Runs Llanbeddau Bric-a-Brac Auction every month because his hammer is the only one loud enough to be heard above all the racquets and arggymentations which is always going on. Also, everyone except John-Willie, the Llanbeddau Cruiser Bruiser, is afraid of him when he loses his rag. When Tammer the Hammer calls hush, by jingo, he do get it.

Usual Pub: Bryn-Tegyll Arms. Captain of Shove Halfpenny Team (Welsh League First Division).

Studies: Authority on habits, ant-ticks, locations, and final desty-nations of rabbits and salmon on moonless nights (all non-acky-demick).

Religion: Sidesman Bethel Chapel, Llanbeddau. Known to be generous to the sick and kneedee. His wife is also said to be a nice little touch. (Source: Charles Delonge-Walker, Knight of the Highway.)

Other: Once won a ten-quid prize in Fishguard when he smashed a pure gold watch to pieces with a 15 lbs pelty hammer being pulled along the top of an anvil at the rate of 1 ft/sec (the watch, not Mr Tammer).

John-Willie

Pugilist of Llanbeddau, West Wales. Formerly the Welsh Destroyer. Currently the Welsh Cruiser Bruiser. In training to become a heavy cruiser bruiser. Perspiring to become a dreadnought with 16-in. biceps. Trained and managed by his big brother Hopkin, who is also his spare ring partner. When J-W is not knocking men down in the ring, he is building them up with PT and weightlifting. (Two bob an hour per pound of flab removed—source: notice on his gym door.)

Nearly got murdered by Morgan Prend y Gast Jenkins, Esq., for punching him during when he was blinking. Morgan re-strained with diffykulty from killing J-W and taken before a beak at the slammer by Tim "The Hammer" Tammer. (Source: Unofficial report not for pubication.)

Defynitions

Manuod y Dref: Town ladies' guild.
Llanbeddau: All-action village of graves.
Charabang: Open-top and open-sided omnibus with solid tyres.

Ogi-Marks: Local name for Cobham marks telling who important was lying under the stone in the old Welsh writing. As most people couldn't understand the angles and strokes, an assentrik old scholar in the village suggested to them what was toffs and keen to be asosiated with their great-ansesters how they could show some importantness by having Maldwyn Bevan ai Fabe, undertakers of all things burial, to write their ogi names on the gravestones, with additional marks to show how big was their funerals. A circle was later added to the ogi-marks to represent Llanbeddau Duck Pond.

9

Well, Stap Me!

Dick: Well, that's what I think, anyway.

Tom: There are alternative views, and what you are saying could be construed in some quarters as utter nonsense!

Dick: What do you mean, nonsense? It's you who's the one who talks drivel around here.

Harry: Oh, I don't know, Dick. Give the poor chap a chance to air his views. Go on, Tom. Let's hear what you've got to say.

Tom: Well, going back to the three Rs again is better than nothing, I suppose.

Dick: Rot! You know damned well that failure to pay attention to them has just about ruined our education system!

Harry: You can't deny that, Tom.

Tom: Of course not. But I believe our learning problem is more fundamental than that.

Dick: What do you mean?

Tom: Well, have you ever considered how unwieldy the way we write really is? If our children were taught shorthand from the word go, they would later have no difficulty whatsoever in taking down dictation, or capturing every word a teacher or university lecturer said, or anything they heard on the radio or TV. The method has been available to us for years, yet we don't avail ourselves of it properly.

Dick: Hmm!

Tom: We must make progress. Look at the Rosetta Stone, for instance. By telling us a little fragment of Egyptian history in three different types of scrip, it allowed Champollion to solve the hieroglyphic alphabet a century ago. We realised at last that the hieroglyphics were actually words and not just pretty designs. It's now obvious to everyone that it would have taken a hundred such stones to say the same thing in the unwieldy picture alphabet of the pharaohs. The Arabs had a lot more sense than us, because when it came to seeking a different form of recording, they chose a type of writing very much akin to shorthand as we know it. You may think that writing from right to left is awkward, but believe me, it is quite natural with the shape of letters they use.

No Arab pupil misses a word in his lectures. He can write like lightning, even faster than our shorthand experts, primarily because he only puts down the consonants and ignores the vowels, which are assumed when read back.

Dick: Well, listen to him! Who would have thought we had a human encyclopaedia in the office!

Harry: Don't be facetious, Dick. I find this interesting. But wouldn't our beautiful language lose something from all this, Tom?

Tom: (Snorting) Nonsense! Ours is a terrible language, a mixture of a load of other languages and full of peculiarities. It is not an easy language to learn properly, even for our people themselves!

Dick: Heavens! That's tantamount to slander—treason! You could have had your ruddy head off for a statement like that a couple of hundred years ago. I'm going. Can't put up with bloody claptrap like that!

Harry: No, hold on. How can you justify what you're saying, Tom?

Tom: Well, if you want a language that's easy to learn and is free of peculiarities and difficulties, you need look no further than Esperanto. It too is a mixture of languages, but when Zamenhof invented it, he was extremely careful to avoid all the pitfalls we encounter in English, French, and German, for instance. It is also a very musical language, sounding very much like Italian. It was very popular before the war, especially in central Europe, and it was also a primary language of the League of Nations in Geneva. The Vatican broadcasts in the language frequently.

Dick: Here we go again! See what I mean?

Harry: No. Go on, Tom.

Tom: Well, I think every child should learn Esperanto as a second language, right from the start of their schooling—a period when it could be absorbed with ease. This should be a requirement of international law. Just imagine how easy world communication would then become.

Dick: I can't believe I'm sitting here listening to all this bull. You'll be rubbishing the three *R*s next, I expect!

Tom: Ha! Arithmetic! Now that's where we really have gone off the rails!

Dick: I suppose you think there's no need to learn such things as the twelve times table!

Tom: As a matter of fact, that's right. You only really need to learn the nine times table. Knowing that, a simple method allows one to find any other value. Believe it or not, a lot of maths can be done in the head without the need for a high IQ.

Dick: Baloney!

Harry: I must say, I agree with Dick on that one.

Tom: Right, well, let me tell you about Professor Trachtenberg—

Dick: Oh hell! No!

Harry: Yes. Go on, Tom. Tell us about him.

Tom: Trachtenberg was a political prisoner of Hitler's regime, and spent six years in solitary confinement in a concentration camp. He was acknowledged to be a fine mathematician. To retain his sanity, he spent his time devising methods whereby quite complicated arithmetic could be done without recourse to paper and pen. When released from captivity, he taught in a school for backward children in Switzerland. Within a few years, his pupils were easily able to outshine the brightest maths children in top-class schools. In parts of America, his methods are very popular indeed. So, chaps, for what my beliefs are worth and to summarise, deep consideration should be given by our education authorities to:

         1. teaching our children to learn shorthand alongside the conventional way we write,

         2. teaching children a universal language from the beginning, and

95

3. familiarising our kids with the Trachtenberg method of mathematics.

Harry: I daresay old Dick here will be loath to admit it, but we've had an eye-opener today, Tom! You've certainly taught us a thing or two, as well as giving us something to think about. Even if your beliefs are somewhat radical, there's no denying the benefits! You know, we really didn't think you had strong feelings about anything, actually!

Tom: Well, neither of you ever bothered to ask, did you?

10

Dr Pelter's Medical

Dr Gerald Pelter was 65 years of age and due for a check-up, so the medical authorities said, so he obediently turned up at the outpatient department of his local hospital on the appointed day. Having been disgustingly fit all his life, he had never had cause to go near such a place, so the experience was new to him. Clutching his briefcase apprehensively, he approached the reception desk and announced his presence to a rather severe-looking lady.

"Er, Doctor Pelter. Gerald Pelter." He smiled, and then as an afterthought, mumbled, "Medical."

The lady smiled back somewhat thinly. At least, he thought it might be a smile. It could, of course, just as well have been a touch of colic, he supposed.

"Ah yes, Doctor." She nodded. "I've been expecting someone. There's quite a crowd coming today, but I think most of them are here now."

Botheration! thought Pelter. *I'm going to be among the last, and I wanted to get to the university early today to prepare things.* He was due to talk at 1400 hrs on "The

Cross-Fertilisation of Periwinkles as a Proven Aid to Stress-Relieving Offshore Safety Officers", a subject dear to his heart.

"Follow me, Doctor," said the lady. She led the way through a warren of corridors to a clinical-looking room, which was tiled to the ceiling. "There's a white coat behind the door there. Here are the thermometers and things, and you'll find some pads, forms, and biros in one of the drawers. Just press the bell when you're ready." And with another colicky smile, she left hurriedly, closing the door behind her.

The good doctor was puzzled. He distinctly recalled a friend telling him that when he'd been up for his medical, they'd told him to "get 'em off". The dragon from reception however, had clearly indicated that he should put more on. He reached behind the door for the coat, concluding that there were probably several stages to be gone through. He supposed that one couldn't easily give coherent answers to questions when starkers—at least, not unless one had plenty of starkers experience.

His friend had also revealed quietly that "they squeeze 'em and say 'cough'", and he hoped that their hands would be warm and they'd be careful. He hadn't forgotten the excruciating pain when Felicity Lewis had done it to him while canoodling in a sidecar behind the school in their teens. She had caused him to jump so vigorously that his head had torn through the canvas hood, and it was only with some difficulty and her assistance that he managed to get it in again. He recalled that the experience had put him off sex for at least a fortnight.

In the middle of this reverie, the door flew open and a similarly clad man rushed in. "Hi there!" he said. "I'm Dr

Brown. Just dashed down to see you're installed OK. Must pop off. Lots to do. See you later!" And he rushed out again.

Oh dear! thought Pelter. *Didn't have a chance to tell him I'm a patient. Must catch him up and explain, or I'll be here till the cows come home.*

Moving rapidly to the door to rectify the situation, he was dismayed to find not a soul in sight. He was certain now that there was something seriously wrong, and he wasn't sure either how he'd got to the room he was in. There seemed to be corridors everywhere. Being a creature of habit who felt distinctly uncomfortable when things became unpredictable, he felt a little panicky.

He moved back into the room and pressed a button on the desk, feeling that this would surely produce someone who could sort things out for him. He then returned to the passage to wait.

Meanwhile, unbeknownst to the preoccupied Pelter, another door in the room had opened. A blowsy, mature-looking female stepped inside in response to a bell in the waiting room. Closing it quietly after her, she disappeared behind a screen just before the doctor returned to the desk, intending to ring for assistance once more. "Come on," he said, glaring at the door. "I haven't got all day!"

A voice from behind the screen said apologetically, "Sorry, Doctor. I'm nearly ready."

Stunned, Pelter strode to the screen and tugged the curtain aside, exposing the lady lying on an examination couch in all her nude splendour!

His pulse rate shot up. In fact, everything shot up. Hastily stepping back, he yanked the curtain shut and stumbled towards the corridor again.

Dr Brown was hurrying to meet him, a worried look on his face. "I say, old man. Awfully sorry and all that. I didn't realise you were in for a check-up. Thought you were the relief doctor—I mean, you being a doctor of sorts as well!"

Pelter was flabbergasted and his blood pressure rocketed even further. *What a damned upstart!* he thought. *It's me who's the real doctor, a doctor of philosophy. I'm one of the finest botanists in Europe and author of several well-known textbooks This young fella is probably a mere bachelor of medicine and surgery or something. Doesn't he know there's one hell of a difference between a bachelor and a PhD? Medical schools might teach them how to fill people up with poisons or cut them to bits, but they seemed to teach them precious little about respect!*

He was on the point of giving forcible voice to his thoughts when it occurred to him that he was not exactly in an advantageous position. The lad would be doing some blood-letting and squeezing any minute and might even want to give him a jab or two.

The intern showed him into another room and, asking Pelter to roll up his sleeve, wrapped his upper arm and began to pump on his sphygmometer.

Systolic 220, diastolic 110. Pulse rate astronomical!

Hell! thought the intern. *This bloke could blow a gasket any minute.* He studied his patient carefully and noted that Pelter did look sort of puce-coloured.

Giving Pelter a shot of a new tranquillizer a medical rep had asked him to try, the intern told him to lie down quietly till he got back and dashed off to another consulting room to see some more patients. Twenty minutes later, he returned and went through the blood-pressure testing procedure again.

Systolic 155, diastolic 90. Pulse rate reasonable.

Cor! What a difference! the intern thought. Damned good stuff, that tranquillizer. The old boy had been in a serious condition a short while ago, and now he was more or less normal for his age. But the intern thought he'd best refer Pelter to his GP for medication all the same.

Having recovered from his unexpected view of the voluptuous female, Pelter had no difficulty in supplying a urine sample, along with some of his blood, which had now gone off the boil. He also managed to blow satisfactory amounts of air down a tube and survived a bashing of his joints by a hammer.

Thanking the youngster, Pelter told him how much he admired his profession. Then, hurrying off to catch a bus to the campus, he reflected on how lucky he had been in electing to take botany at college. He was fairly certain after this recent experience that had he become a medico instead, he'd have been stone cold dead long ago!

11

She Was a Terrible Bore

One of the ladies in Marion's group of friends was rather well off and was clothes mad. She spent a fortune on the most expensive garments and rarely wore them more than three times before they were discarded to charity.

Now although ladies love to go around the establishments that cater for them, there is a limit. After a while, the girls got fed up.

Their loved ones had their own lads' meetings every Tuesday in the comfort of Sainsbury's Restaurant. The envious fed-upness of their wives eventually came up in the conversation one week when the clothes-mad woman's husband wasn't present.

Being a wicked bunch when they were not putting the world to rights, they decided to play a prank on the lady in question and concocted a flyer which would be delivered to her by mail. This is how it read:

Imran's Mobile Boutique
(Incorporated in Pakistan)
Branches in Jaipur, Karachi, and Cardiff

Esteemed Lady,

We thank you most respectably for your expected custom. Be insured, we have your valued money at heart, offering best female "Haute Couture" goods from our mills for your delight. All our cloth has been naturally sun-bleached on the banks of the sacred Ganges and washed in its waters for super cleanliness and to reduce shrinkage to minimum.

This is, good lady, more than 100 per cent guarantee.

We learn from internet databank you are renowned purchaser of fine clothes. Accordingly, our mobile boutiquemobile which is now in your area will call on you at:

50 Birkley Close, Mayals,
Swansea, West Glamshire

You can peruse at uttermost discretion and leisure all ten racks of our exalted goods and lingerie fitted with world's best-known name labels. (These can be quickly changed on dresses or transferred from your cast-offs on request as you wait.)

Look out breathlessly for our discreet visit to your home All our vans are furniture-size for your comfort and have name Imran on them with our national elephant picture for your immediate identification.

(Note: We are only calling daylightly. Strictly cash. Please have purse ready.)

If your wardrobe is presently full or, dear lady, you are not currently interested in our top fashion lines, please to inform Karachi 00871-3224-11397 (only 288p/min) and tell Jemima you are not wanting. She is uttering most well in English and can take orders from you far and wide.

Perhaps you like to have friends in the house when we call so that they know you have quality taste. Make them sickly with envy from you!

All our boutiquemobiles are fitted with heated changing room.

(Old rags from Eastex, Windsmor, Country Casuals, Gucci, Van Graff, Frascatti, La Tous Boulay, Roebucks, Spears and Jackson, Madame Foner, etc. partly exchanged. Please do not remove labels. We have trained expertise in this art and can recycle.)

Note: We promise that all purchases thoroughly deloused before leaving our factory. Topmost and bottommost satisfaction guaranteed. You will be itching muchly for us to call again.

Finally, dear lady, what a surprise we are having for you when you buy one of our haute coutures. We will enter your esteemed name in our Karachi raffle! This is a trip to the Baba Wagit Temple by bicycle cart. All air trip costs prepaid—by you.

Enjoy an afternoon in the boutiquemobile and be impressed by a discreet and private view of Imran's acclaimed gear.

Well, we all waited breathlessly for an explosion to occur, but nothing happened. She had obviously decided not to show it to anyone, as she was not exactly the type of person who could take this sort of joke kindly.

However, a few weeks later, there was a suppressed giggle among the girls when she casually asked if any of the ladies had had any flyers lately. Surprise, surprise, no; they didn't know what she was talking about. Had she had one, then? What did it have to say?

"Oh, nothing much," she replied. "It was just about holiday trips to Pakistan."

12

A Welcome Arrest

My friend George was going back from the Canary Islands to the UK for a short holiday and was looking forward to it very much. He would stay in his son's home in Kingston. His lad, who was a police officer in the Met in London, had promised to pick him up at the airport and drive him there.

On the eve of arrival, the policeman got a few hours off and returned to his quarters to change and get his father's ETA and airline details. To his dismay, he couldn't find the vital piece of paper. Reversing his beloved Astra GTi out of the car park, he headed for Heathrow. Dashing into the arrivals hall of one of the terminals, he approached the assistant at the information desk. "Excuse me, love. When do you expect the next couple of charter flights in from Tenerife?"

"Never!" was the terse reply.

"What do you mean by 'never'?" enquired the puzzled cop.

"Just what she said, pal," butted in her male companion. "Never! Charters don't come to Heathrow—they go to Gatwick!"

Turning away in disgust, the policeman pondered his next move and, thrusting his hands into his pockets, found the paper he'd been looking for. "Darn it! It is Gatwick. It's flight 479, and it's going to land in about ten minutes' time."

Returning to the Information Desk, the cop collared the man again and told him he wanted a call sent to Gatwick Arrivals Information.

"Sorry, pal. We don't do things like that. Try calling them from one of those phone booths over there."

The policeman did, but the booths were all occupied, and each had a queue waiting to use the phone within. So he went back to the information desk again. Reaching into an inside pocket of his suit, he produced his warrant card and flashed it in the info chap's face. "Listen, chum. There's not a hope of using any of those phones immediately, as each one's got a queue a mile long. Now, there's a prisoner on flight 479, which is arriving at Gatwick very, very shortly. If you don't get me through to them quickly, you can count yourself in plenty of trouble, and probably out of a job. So move!"

The man hadn't worked there long and wasn't sure what he should do in such circumstances. The cop certainly didn't sound as though he was joking. The man reached for his phone, rang Gatwick, and, getting them right away, handed the set to the policeman.

"Hello!" said a voice. "Gatwick Arrivals here. Can I help you?"

"This is a Metropolitan police officer phoning from Heathrow. Look. You've got a Mr Hamlyn arriving shortly from Tenerife on flight 479, and we want him badly. Do everything you can to keep him at your desk or in the terminal building till we can get a detective to you to pick him up. He mustn't have any idea that we're after him, so don't mention the police on any account and don't bring your own police into it. Tell him a yarn about some friends phoning up to say that they've arranged a party for him. They're sorry to be late, but their chauffeur will pick him up in just over half an hour. Do you understand?"

The chap on the other end of the line said he did. He wondered as he put the phone down why the Gatwick police couldn't be trusted with the arrest of the crook. Funny people, the Met!

The Astra GTi went down the M25 like a rocket. At the terminal, the info man, seeing the 479 passengers coming out of the customs hall, sent out a call for our passenger in question, George.

George emerged from the exit and immediately scanned the crowd at the barrier for signs of his boy. He couldn't see him. He was slowing down his trolley to give the lad a better chance to spot him, when he heard his name blaring over the tannoy and a request to go to the information desk in the main hall.

He hurried over to the desk and made himself known. As the man gave him the message, George kept looking to left and to right for signs of his lad—looks that the man took to be the typical furtive glances of the born crook.

George was understandably puzzled. Who on earth, apart from his son, knew he was coming? And a party with a chauffeur to pick him up? It was all a bit too ostentatious for his taste. He asked the desk man to check that he'd got the right message.

"You're Mr George Hamlin, aren't you, sir?"

George agreed.

"Then the message is definitely for you. I've got it on computer too. Sound's all very nice to me, sir. Why don't you have a drink at the bar across the hall while you wait? They shouldn't be all that long."

George had to admit that after the four-hour trip in the plane, this watering hole certainly looked attractive. It was also well situated for him to keep an eye on everyone coming into the terminal. It was likewise well situated for the info man to keep a careful watch on the thug.

Half an hour later, George was beginning to wonder what had happened to his son and to the chauffeur of his mysterious friends. Then one of his arms was roughly grabbed from behind, and a familiar voice whispered, "Don't look back, Dad. Just come quietly and scowl at that chap who's looking pleased with himself on the information desk. Sorry I'm late. I went to the wrong darned airport!"

Frog-marching George before him and twisting his arm well up his back so that he was virtually helpless, the policeman grinned as he went past the info man and gave him a thumbs-up sign with his free hand. Then, directing a porter to bring the trolley after them to the car park, he said, "Come on. Let's get to hell out of here before someone smells a rat. Arresting you was the only way I could be sure of not missing you. I'll explain it all in the car!"

13

Wartime Scouts

Except for one or two angels, the members of the Thirty-Third Swansea Bonymaen Scout Troop were all baddies, having been recruited from his throng by the senior probation officer of the city—a keen scouter. By a combination of the example set by the goodies, and the possibility of an official degree of forgiveness on the part of the scoutmaster, it was hoped that the irresponsible hellions would eventually change for the better. And so indeed it proved to be!

Healthy outdoor weekends, interesting projects, and responsibility also helped to do the trick. Almost without exception, as I remember, the lads ultimately turned into nearly model citizens.

When it came to inter-troop competitions, they had a bit of a reputation as "toughies" to keep up, and invariably came out on top at football, boxing, and other physical games. They were seldom behind at bridge-building, woodsmanship, trekking, and good outdoor scouting generally. It's only fair to say, though, that the scoutmaster used this reputation thing for all it was worth. He got them to work really hard as a troop to maintain it, so that half the time, the other troops were beaten before they had even locked horns with us!

Having been formed in the war, the Thirty-Third were not all that well off. We used to have to borrow heavy stuff like a trek cart, boilers, pots, pans, and tents from more prosperous but less motivated outfits, who also tended not to argue too much when we asked for their help.

There was one rule, however, that I recollect the troop observing meticulously. Borrowed equipment was always returned "as was" or even better. The only time I can recall our nearly failing to observe this tenet was not, in fact, through any fault of ours.

We had just tugged a cart up a steep slope near a place called Ystradgynlais, close to the head of the Swansea valley. After a short breather, we commenced our descent on the other side. The cart was laden with camping gear, surmounted by Garry Pew, who hung on precariously, claiming to be suffering agonies from blistered feet.

The cart was rocking about alarmingly, barely under control, when we were passed by an American army convoy. The Yanks enjoyed taking the mickey out of us in a friendly sort of way, which we didn't mind all that much, particularly as they threw us packs of gum and some Lucky Strikes. These were deftly caught by Garry Pew, who managed to secrete some of the gum before we could stop and get our hands on him.

The strain of having to haul the heavy cart up a steep hill, followed by the effort needed to prevent it running away the other side, was beginning to tell. We were discussing the advisability of stopping for tea and a bite to eat when along came another American dodge.

The truck was moving very fast, probably trying to catch up with the convoy. Its driver blew his klaxon as he passed us. The noise was so unexpectedly loud and the truck so close that the boys between the shafts of the cart veered sharply to the near side of the road, while those on the outside let go of the restraining ropes in alarm.

The result was disastrous. As the truck disappeared out of sight around a bend, the driver unaware of the consequences of his action, the near-side shaft hit the side of a low, walled bridge and snapped like a carrot, sending Garry Pew flying over the parapet into the river below.

With an effort, he made it to the bank, where he was fished out by willing hands. The scoutmaster didn't quite know whether to award him a flying badge or one for swimming efficiency. In the end he decided Gary should have neither, as he had got his feet blistered and caused the troop some inconvenience.

One of the chaps between the shafts had been run over by a cart wheel. He was in some pain, having sustained two cracked ribs and a broken nose. However, such was the care and attention lavished on him by two members of his patrol, who had been studying for weeks for their first aid badges, that they were awarded these. Accolades were given for performance "in the field", so to speak, or rather on the side of the road near Ystradgynlais.

The two fledgling paramedics were delighted. But they had to wait nearly three months for the new badges to join the already imposing array on their shirt sleeves. The production of scout badges didn't have a particularly high priority in the war effort.

Almost all of our subscription money saved thus far went into replacing some badly dented pans and replacing a broken shaft, which was quite a setback for us. We had been looking forward to buying our own gear and becoming independent of other troops in the town.

Then our fortunes changed. Three of our baddies appeared to revert to type and arrived at a meeting one night with some six-man tents and all the fittings, which they insisted they saw "fall off the back of a lorry". As a goodie, it was some time later that I got to know the meaning of those words.

One weekend, we went up a local mountain in response to a farmer's request to augment the woodcutting and land drainage work of some Italian prisoners of war. Our job was to make wooden bridges over gullies that the Italians had dug to run drainage water off the mountain. For this service, the farmer undertook to supply us with eggs and milk free of charge.

Two of us were in the same private school as the farmer's son and daughter. The farmer casually mentioned to the scoutmaster one day that his son was being subject to bullying there. The skipper quizzed us in front of him, and we admitted that we were aware of it.

Looking at us meaningfully, he told the farmer that the Thirty-Third knew their duty. He was certain that the trouble would cease forthwith. "You shepherd that lad," he said to us, "or there's no further promotion for you lot." Thus, young Tom began to enjoy his schooling with two Thirty-Third heavies as his pals.

A month later, his father expressed his great relief, and we were treated to free bacon with our milk and eggs. Shortly afterwards, his son was recruited into the troop and was hardened up to the point that he became quite good at looking after himself and no longer suffered molestation.

———————————◆ ◦ ◆——————————

Another bonus proved invaluable to us and went a long way to the scoutmaster attaining his principal goal: the farmer gave us unlimited use of the surrounding woodland for camping purposes, as long as we undertook to do a little maintenance work on each of our visits. It was a lucrative reciprocal agreement for both parties. As his son joined us on every trip, we were never short of fresh farm bread, butter, honey, and cheese—things almost impossible to get at home, short of being in hospital or borstal. The members of the Thirty-Third were very reluctant to miss one of these trips.

Often when going on long weekend camps up this mountain, my kit was rather more special than the rest. This came about because I had passed the signalling course and was given the responsibility of looking after the troop crystal set and aerial. With this valuable apparatus, we were able to keep in touch with the fast-moving events in the outside world.

The set consisted of a box containing a coil on a glass tube, over the top of which was a brass bar holding a metal slide. On the underside of the box lid was a small glass bottle containing a crystal and a cat's whisker made of platinum wire—two vital components of first-generation radios. Other vital parts were two terminals, one for the earth and the other for the aerial, which was a large roll of copper wire about 70 feet long which I had to sling between trees.

Adjustment of the apparatus called for some very delicate tweaking, which I was considered good at. Sound came from a pair of ex U-boat headphones, which a gentleman in the village had recovered from a German vessel during the 1914–18 war and had kindly donated to us.

I had just picked up the nine o'clock news one night and was informing the skipper—who was sitting around the campfire with the lads—that our army had recaptured Tobruk from Hitler's Afrika Korps, when the sirens went off in the town below the mountain, heralding an air raid.

The dull throbbing sound of Junkers and Dornier bombers could be heard approaching in the distance. Searchlights stabbed the sky in search of them, while the city's barrage balloons climbed rapidly into the air to provide the docks and factories with a forest of steel cables.

The Thirty-Third went into a well-rehearsed wartime drill. Lining up at ease on either side of the fire, two patrols peed on it to put it out, the third patrol standing by in case we failed. We all then dived into one of the nearest gullies, there to take shelter till the Jerries had gone and the all-clear siren had sounded.

When a new troop was formed in our school and numbered the Thirty-Seventh Swansea troop, my brother and I joined. Being experienced scouters, we were soon made patrol leaders, he taking over the Robins and me the Bulldogs.

We wondered at first whether we could enjoy the luxury of belonging to two troops, as it stretched our meagre assets to the limits. But we found that by sacrificing one of Eynon's pies and one of Joe's ice cream parlour coffee dashes once a week, we could still appear loyal to our alma mater while still maintaining our stronger links with the most macho troop in town.

The Thirty-Seventh consisted of lads from other troops in Carmarthen, Gorseinon, Gower, and elsewhere. It could be said to be quite a skilful lot. The skipper was our Latin master. There could not have been many troops who, around their campfire, enjoyed quizzes containing questions such as "what is the genitive of *dominus*?" A wrong answer would guarantee you detention in camp, keeping the fires lit, while the rest of the troop were off enjoying themselves.

One of our first jobs of any consequence came along soon after the troop's formation. The school had been burgled on two successive nights. The headmaster thought it would be a jolly good idea to station two of the patrols in the grounds for a couple of nights a week.

Two boys stayed for three hours at a time in the staff room, with a whistle. The rest slept in a tent in the garden, opposite the head's room. The troop leader acted much like an orderly corporal in the army and was provided with an alarm clock, so that the guard changes were made on time. None of us got a lot of sleep; however, it was all too exciting.

The headmaster took the precaution of mentioning our presence to the local police sergeant. This worthy decided on our first night to look in and satisfy himself that all was OK.

Now the sergeant had never been in the scouts or in the army, and was therefore not conversant with the number of trip hazards around even the simplest of tents. He fell over two guy ropes in an effort to find the entrance to the tent, bringing all the lads inside awake. Though scared almost witless, we unsheathed our scout knives and prepared to battle with the burglars.

John Stanley was nearest the door when the sergeant poked his head through the flap. He had taken off his steel helmet to get through, and received a lump the size of an egg on his forehead with our peg mallet. The heavy policeman collapsed on top of us, out for count.

A quick flash with a torch showed us the enormity of the trouble we were in, and we looked to our troop leader for direction. Fair play to the poor boy: he knew what we had to do, even though our instincts told us to run like—like the dickens. Blowing his whistle to call the chaps in the staffroom, he gathered us all outside the tent. Picking up the heavy sergeant, we carried him out of the school gates and onto the road, intending to take him to Swansea General Hospital a couple of hundred yards away.

Two men were approaching us in the dim light, pushing a wheelbarrow. Taking in what we were doing, they offered to help. The troop leader thanked them but declined their offer, as he had all his chaps on the job and would be able to get the bobby down to the hospital without any trouble.

This was fine by the two kind gentlemen, who watched us disappear before doing the school for the third night running.

About the Author

Dr Sims is the author of *A Cambrian Kaleidoscope* and *Taffs Abroad*, along with numerous technical works. On retirement, he decided to try his hand at writing about some of his experiences in the Middle and Far East as well as the UK. He currently lives in the Mayals, Swansea, flies model aircraft, and studies his native language.

Lightning Source UK Ltd.
Milton Keynes UK
UKHW041149121218
333839UK00001B/15/P

9 781728 380490